Coffee

&

Conversations

Author

Ron Botha

First published 2021

Unless otherwise stated all biblical quotes are taken from the NIV version of the Bible, Copyright 1973, 1974, 1984 by International Bible Society.

Format and Edited by **Bonita J Solomons**

Book cover and graphic designer **Candice Botha**

ISBN: 978 9935 24907 4

TABLE OF CONTENTS

THANKS AND ACKNOWLEDGEMENTS

I wish to thank everyone who contributed to the original Facebook poll with memorable and life changing quotes by Alfie Fabe.

Special thanks go to my family, Anne, Candice, Keenan and Kay-Lynn for their invaluable input in knit-picking, editing and general design.

"We make an awesome team".

INTRODUCTION

The modern Christian world has been saturated with books, blogs, videos, and online material about achieving success in ministry and performing excellently in one's
corner of the vineyard. Much of this material is authored by leaders who have done well and are now sharing the principles that got them to that level. The information age allows the world to peek into their success stories, which immediately conjures a desire to reach a similar achievement in a shorter space of time. What most folk do not fully realise is that many of these leaders only reached their pinnacle of success in the latter part of their lives. Many of them started their journeys being severely disadvantaged and they had to fight relentlessly to achieve even minute victories. They had to develop
important virtues like patience, tenacity, and resilience in the process.

While all this material and information is good, there is very little out there that actually deal with things leaders face every day. Having a successful ministry is one thing but being a leader in a post-modern world is quite another. Also, there is very little material that speaks to leaders on the other side of the tracks. Let's face it, there are millions of leaders across the world that do not have access to the information that other more
connected leaders have. Many of them have not grown up in church neither have they been to the fancy seminaries that most western Pastors have had the privilege of being trained at. Since many of these new leaders are first generation preachers, they may not have had mentors who walked with them. The

truth for many of them is that they were thrust into leadership because there was a great need, and they did so without a voice of wisdom to guide them along the way.

My name is Ron, and my wife and I had the distinct privilege to be mentored by one of the great leaders of my time and even though I was a graduate of a prestigious Seminary in South Africa, the greatest transition in my life took place in the twenty three years that I sat at his feet. Our relationship was so intimate that I prefer to call him my spiritual father. His name was Alfred Gerald Fabe, and this book is written in his memory as he transitioned to glory on 30 July 2020, four months before its completion.

As its title suggests, this book is about the conversations Alfie had with the many spiritual sons and daughters he mentored. Many of those conversations took place in coffee shops and restaurants all over Cape Town, or around the world. They were often intense, thought provoking, inducing painful paradigm shifts. How can I forget that pensive yet loving look in his eyes as he would whip out his pen, grab the nearest serviette (napkin) and write his thoughts on it. Many of the quotations in this book were indeed those thoughts transferred onto serviettes or pieces of paper and it would not be surprising if these could still be found in someone's study. I still have one.

This book contains some of the vital things he deposited in my life and it is written in a way that would help every Christian leader, whether seasoned or aspiring, navigate through some of the tough things in the ministry.

Have you ever been to the place in your leadership journey where you asked hard questions about methods and motivations for doing things, yet because you did not find suitable answers you just carried on as normal, even though you were uncomfortable? Oh, that happened to me more times than I remember.

In this book I will walk you through some of those important things about ministry in the twenty first century that you may not find in the curriculum of the seminary near you. This book will help you see the value of relationships and why it is foundational to everything that happens in ministry. It will look at some of the real battles we face and how they are best won.

The subjects of accountability and transparency are hard pills to swallow for some, but there is a unique way this can work for everybody and I will reveal how this comes about and is maintained.

Is leadership about getting your point across and getting people to follow you or is there a hidden lesson Jesus tried to convey in the way He modelled leadership? There are some pertinent things I wish to convey to you that will change the way you lead.

Finally, this book will not be complete without addressing the current crisis and how we traverse it before casting our eyes on a world beyond COVID 19.

Most of these teachings are preceded by and based on the statements Alfie made. These statements he not only repeated endlessly, but also lived them, until I grasped them and made the transition to live them too.

Alfie Fabe said: ***"Some things are better caught than taught"***. My prayer is that the precepts I develop in this book may not be mere information that you absorb, but real life changing principles that equip you for the next season of ministry.

Chapter one

"It doesn't happen at this church".

-Alfred Gerald Fabe

Early beginnings

I recently viewed the movie entitled, *"I can only imagine"*, and I was moved by the story of musician and song writer Bart Millard who suffered physical and emotional abuse at the hands of his father. The love of God found them both on separate occasions and embarked them on a journey of forgiveness and repentance until they reconciled.

There are many incredible redemption stories all around us. My personal story does not fit the dramatic pattern of these and other stories, but there is a common denominator that runs through them all. It features the love of a Father, who extends His divine grace to all of mankind, leading them to repentance and faith in Christ, and the promise of abundant living.

I was born into a fairly conservative Christian family. At age 14, I surrendered my life to Christ at a Baptist youth camp. Over the next 13 years I served in various capacities in that denomination until I heard the Lord calling me to full time ministry. After leaving Seminary I was honoured to serve as a Baptist minister for the next 6 years. During that time, I was part of a fraternal of Baptist ministers who received the Baptism in the Holy Spirit. This was the experience that changed everything for me.

At the end of our sixth year, Anne and I, after much prayer and counsel, decided to leave the church we had pastored and plant a non-denominational church. The new church was an exciting venture and a few months into the journey we began seeking for an organisation that could provide us with spiritual oversight. After checking out a few organisations, my dad connected us with a pastor that had been visiting some of the *Holy Spirit* meetings he was hosting. This pastor was indeed Alfie Fabe, and I was about to embark on one of the greatest journeys of my life.

At the time I was a young, arrogant preacher desperately in need of a mentor. I was honoured to walk with Alfie for 23 years and in that time, I went through some painful, yet crucial paradigm shifts that began to shape me in ways I never thought possible. This chapter is devoted to some of those initial shifts in my perspective which affected my approach to ministry in the future.

Alfie Fabe often used a phrase in jest during his sermons when referring to some of the foolish things leaders did. He would say *"it doesn't happen at this church"*. While some people giggled there was always a sense of conviction, because in the audience there would either be a victim or a perpetrator of some type of outrageous behaviour. But he didn't just leave it there. Every time he spoke to his leaders corporately or privately, he used the opportunity to talk about some of these foolish and unbiblical things.

I wish to draw attention to a few of those things in this chapter, based on the things he said to me in our conversations over coffee.

The dangers of institutionalism.

The story of the church is indeed an interesting one. After the upper room event on the day of Pentecost, the church grew rapidly in Jerusalem. It is important to understand that the religious atmosphere in Jerusalem was Jewish with some Graeco-Roman influence. Apart from the travelling of Jesus there was no place of worship connected to this new phenomenon called Christianity. The conversion of 3000 people in one day, followed by a continuous growth the days and weeks following was nothing short of a miracle. That type of supernatural experience would be called 'revival' by people who study divine moves of the spirit.

The Bible then talks about the church moving from house to house and having fellowship daily, breaking bread, praying, and rejoicing.

Acts 2:46-47 [46] *Every day they continued to meet together in the temple courts. They broke bread in their homes and ate together with glad and sincere hearts,*
[47]*praising God and enjoying the favor of all the people. And the Lord added to their number daily those who were being saved.*

This was indeed the trend that God intended. In fact, as the church grew the apostles in Jerusalem tried to keep this new move of God localized. This was not the plan of God, and after Stephen preached that powerful sermon in *Acts 7*, the Jews became so incensed with the truth of his words that they grabbed hold of him and stoned him. He became the first martyr and almost immediately a great persecution broke out in Jerusalem. As a result, the believers fled for their lives because the Jews and the Romans were intent on destroying this very thing that evoked so much attention and drew so many people away from their traditional religious observances. The authorities also felt that this new, fast growing movement was becoming a political threat to the Roman empire because the word 'Kingdom' was often used in their speech.

Christians, on the other hand, must have felt that this was the end of their short lived joy, but God had other plans.
The interesting thing is that wherever people went they could not contain this newfound joy and so they ignited people where they landed. As a result, the Gospel reached the parts of Asia minor wherever Christians of the diaspora landed.

Paul (formerly known as Saul) was a major instigator in the persecution of the Christians. The first time he is mentioned in the Bible, he was present at the stoning of Stephen (*Acts 7*). He was part of the crowd, approving that murderous act. Well, two chapters later, after climbing the ranks in the "Jewish Gestapo", he had an encounter with Jesus on the road to Damascus that changed his life forever. He became an apostle to the very people that he had been trying to eliminate. As a result, the Gospel reached Asia minor in a very short time.

When you read the letters of Paul you find that he did numerous trips, sometimes visiting the same city on more than one occasion and staying in the city for extensive periods of time, discipling the church and raising leaders. The church grew in leaps and bounds just as God intended. I honestly believe this was the model God had intended when He first poured out His Spirit on the day of Pentecost. This was indeed the case for the first few hundred years of church history. There were major theological debates that took place between the church fathers yes, but the church continued to grow from strength to strength, until an emperor by the name of Constantine the Great came to power. He ruled from 306 to 327 AD. In 318 AD he decided that the church should not be meeting in homes and he granted the church their first Cathedrals. As soon as this happened, the church seemed to fall into a state of slumber.

In my lifetime I have been involved in planting a few churches and I also worked closely with Pastors who were church planters. I noticed the same trend repeat itself. While the church met in homes and other temporary places, growth seemed to be unprecedented. Once the church acquired property, the focus shifted from evangelism and the principles of ministry to the furnishing of a building. The church focussed itself on its own activities and no longer enjoyed vigorous growth. Consequently, the enthusiasm of the people began to wane, and growth was stunted.

The church in the time of Constantine became institutionalized and all sorts of legalism entered the assembly, resulting in the impending dark ages which lasted a millennium, until the time of Martin Luther, the great reformer. By that time, the church became an organisation which required people to be subject to all forms of legal requirements for membership. Martin Luther's theses may have sparked the great reformation, but it certainly did not remove the legalism associated with belonging to an assembly of believers. In fact, as the denominations developed from that point on, the legal requirements for membership became even greater.

Both Alfie Fabe and I came from denominations that had their own distinctives. Some of which were not even rooted in scripture but were placed there to adhere to the political climate of the day, or simply to control the clergy or laity.

One of the hardest things that happened in our relationship was the process of ridding me of that paradigm. I wanted to place regulations around everything. I had adopted a constitution and by-laws that looked like a law book.
Institutionalism does not promote growth. In fact, institutionalism opposes growth because it is a system adopted to control those that adhere to it.

What is denominationalism?

The word denomination really means division. In financial terms it means the classification/dividing of money into size or value.

This definition by Jerald C Brauer seems to sum it up.
"The system and ideology founded on the division of the religious population into numerous ecclesiastical bodies, each stressing particular values or traditions and each competing with the other in the same community under substantial conditions of freedom" (Jerald C. Brauer, Ed., The Westminster Dictionary of Church History, Philadelphia: The Westminster Press, 1971, pp. 262-263).

What are the dangers of denominationalism?

People find their identity in their denomination rather than in Christ. They would rather say "I am Baptist or Methodist or Pentecostal" than "I follow Christ".

Church is always associated with a building than with the true *Ekklesia*. People are taught to go to church rather than be the church. People rely on rituals, customs, and traditions, rather than revelation for knowing Christ. The congregation is denominationally minded rather than kingdom focussed. People from different denominations do not partner together in a kingdom based project.

Denominations encourage the idea that it is healthy to differ on major points of doctrine. People interpret the Bible through the lens of their denominational tenets and ignore the context and teachings of scripture. For example, my belief that the Baptism by the Holy Spirit into the body of Christ, and the Baptism in the Holy Spirit as essentially being the same thing was based on my denominational tenets of faith. In hindsight I do not believe in lawlessness, nor will I ever. I believe in having healthy structures that will prevent lawlessness. However, those structures should always promote evangelism and turn every member into a minister.

This brings me to my next point:

"Organisations are not God's idea, people are".

-Alfred Gerald Fabe

When God birthed the church on the day of Pentecost, He never had an organisation in mind. In fact, that was the understanding all over the New Testament. Letters were never written to churches with fancy names as we see today.

Alfie Fabe and I visited a country in Africa in 2003 and we were amazed at the names given to churches. Just about every conceivable phrase in the New Testament had become the name of a church and to be fancy, some even placed the word 'International' at the end. There were tens of thousands of churches scattered all over the city. Now just imagine, each church had a constitution and a different way to control their people.

When Paul wrote letters to the churches, he never wrote a single letter to a specific church with a fancy name. In fact, all the believers meeting in a city were called the church of that city e.g., the churches of Ephesus, Galatia, and Corinth for example simply referred to the believers who resided in those cities.

What does that tell us? It simply means that organisations were never God's idea. People were His great idea. God gave His Son to die for people not organisations. When Jesus ascended into Heaven, He released gifts upon people not upon organisations. Power for ministry was released upon people. Throughout the Bible God spoke to His people. He is a personal God. God invests only in His people.

Jesus spent his ministry time on earth investing in a group of men, whom He was going to later entrust with His church. His intention was that the same pattern be followed today.

Every minister must understand this principle for any ministry to be successful. The bulk of the leader's time and energy should be spent in investing in the people.

Every modern leadership guru will categorically state that the most valuable resource of any organisation is the people. Without the people, an organisation cannot survive. As a result, the most successful organisations today spend the maximum amount of money, time and effort investing in their staff.

Alfie Fabe truly lived for his people. The bulk of his time was spent investing in his leaders and in those whom he was mentoring for leadership. The problem with having a big church is that one cannot spend time with everyone. I listened to an interview on podcast recently. The interviewee had left a mega-church. He mentioned that in the five years that he had served that church as a volunteer, he never had the opportunity to get close to his pastor, because he was always too busy. I listened to another podcast on leadership and the pastor being interviewed made it clear that he does not easily meet with someone. In fact, his schedule is so hectic that he can only field brief telephone calls at a weeks' notice.

Do not assume any clerical title or office mentioned in *Ephesians 4:11,* if you are not interested in investing maximum time with people, because that is what ministry encompasses. People are God's idea, and they should become ours too. Organisations cannot provide the safety net every minister needs.

My experience in the institutionalised church has been a valuable one because it allowed me to view close, the abuse of power very often wielded by boards and committees. I cannot

begin to describe the countless times people left a meeting with the church board more distraught than before.
My spiritual dad taught me that every minister needs a safety net into which he or she can fall when trouble occurs. This presupposes that every one of us will make huge errors in ministry.

The great Apostle Peter, who told Jesus that he would always be at His side, denied being a part of Him the moment things got tough for him. That must have been a disappointment when Jesus was at His most vulnerable and He wanted his closest friends to stand with Him. He had just been arrested and was about to appear before Pilate. The Roman soldiers were aggressive in their quest to arrest anyone who was part of the entourage of Jesus and at the time when He needed Peter to provide the emotional and moral support He needed as a man, Peter decided to distance himself from Jesus, at least when questioned.

I do not have enough fingers to count the many times I let my family, the church and God down with my impulsiveness and stubbornness and I should probably not be in ministry today if an institution had their way with me. A glance at the constitution of any institutionalised church will reveal the lack of or absence of grace contained in the disciplinary clauses. Of course, there should be regulations that prescribe our demeanour in ministry. However, when the execution of these regulations is devoid of grace then disaster looms and our church meetings become nothing other than courtrooms, where the guilty are often judged with vengeance and hostility. God's plan for His people is that our fellowship with each other should provide a safety net wherein we can land when trouble comes, because trouble will come.

Romans 14:17 *For the kingdom of God is not a matter of eating and drinking, but of righteousness, peace, and joy in the Holy Spirit.*

Notice the balance here. When dealing with a brother or sister who has sinned, we have a duty to deal with matters righteously, but our pursuit of righteousness should always end in joy and peace. This is Kingdom living. When people sin, they should not be running away from the church, for that is what the enemy wants them to do. The devil wants to get them away from the fellowship of the saints at all costs. Instead, they should be running towards the church.

Some years ago, in one of the first churches I pastored, a woman walked into my office and reported a crime that one of our members committed. It was a heinous crime that led to arrest and incarceration. Fortunately, bail was granted, and he was released pending trial. I was approached by his attorney to testify on his behalf, which I did. The judge seemed to be aware of traditional church disciplinary measures and enquired from me what procedures I would put in place to discipline him post sentencing. He particularly asked me if he would be allowed to participate in the Lord's supper. The trend in most churches was that the offender would be disallowed to participate in the Lord's supper for a stipulated period of time, as a form of punishment. I broke that trend that day and I told the Judge that he would not be shunned from the Lord's table. However, he would have to be at every worship service and every Bible study and prayer meeting, additionally he would meet with me once per week. Confused, the Judge enquired why I would pursue this course of action. I told him that when any of my children sin, I do not punish them by making them skip a meal. Every son deserved dinner, regardless of his misdemeanour.

Well, I pursued that course of action just as I promised the judge and this brother was not left to feel as an outcast, but as one of the saints. We provided care and counseling and within a few months he was restored and walking with Jesus again. Even though the church had a rigid constitution, I fought for the safety net and despite the sceptical comments and glances I received from that day on, this brother was restored and that was all that mattered.

I will talk more about the features of this safety net in the next chapter.

I now wish to raise an issue that does not relate to the ones I dealt with earlier in this chapter. It has to do with what happens when we discover a truth or experience a new move of God. This was indeed one of the first truths my spiritual father taught me.

"When God restores a truth to the body of Christ, the tendency of the church is to take that truth to the extreme".

-Alfred Gerald Fabe

The character of God is utterly amazing. Even though He does not change according to the scriptures, we never find God doing the same thing twice. This part of His character is fascinating. God never dealt with two people the same way.   Also, God works according to the seasons of our lives. There are things God will not give us in early seasons, which He will grant us in later seasons. That's all related to His Omniscience. He is sovereign and does everything in accordance with His perfect will.

There are times in the life of a church when God restores a truth in relation to their growth in a season. The problem is not the revelation of that truth but what the church does with it. One of the problems is not knowing how to apply that truth in its context and in accordance with the Word of God.

When I served as the director of the fellowship of churches and ministries, I was part of, my secretary would schedule preaching or visiting appointments at those churches, which usually happened twice per month. On one occasion, I was scheduled to preach at one of our churches and as usual I made sure that I had met the pastor before the service. Upon meeting him I noticed that his demeanour was rather stiff and starchy. He was wearing a clerical robe and duly informed me that they were observing the Lord's supper that day. Being a small church, they met in a temporary makeshift building in his backyard. The service went well until the time came for the Lord's supper. Suddenly buckets of water were brought and before I knew it everyone's feet were washed. As a matter of fact, someone was delegated to share a devotion on why a foot-washing ceremony was necessary at every communion service. His reason was simple...because Jesus did it in *John 13*.

Now it was obvious that God spoke to them from this passage at some time but after this revelation they needed to ask God for wisdom in applying the principles of servant-hood in every-day life. Churches and ministers do this all the time.

Two of the modern forms of extremism is centred around the prophetic and apostolic gifts. In the 80s, God restored the

prophetic gift to its fullness (at least in our neck of the woods) and suddenly prophets were coming out of the woodwork and extremism ensued. Certain churches had a leaning only to the prophetic and the balance of ministry was lost in the process. This led to gross abuse of the gift because if someone said that he/she heard from God, no one was qualified enough to raise any questions or call them to correction.
Papa Fabe sadly was called into many of these situations where individuals had been horribly abused by "prophets" with no integrity or even knowledge about the use of their gifting.

There are three passages in the New Testament that deal with the prophetic.

The first is in **Romans 12:6** where the prophetic gift is dealt with as a motivational gift or the gift we are given at conversion. This simply means that your primary gift is hearing from God and conveying that message to God's people in obedience. Notice I said in obedience. There are many times God speaks to prophets, but He does not tell them to convey what He said. It simply means they must pray. Prayer and obedience are the difference between a word spoken to edify and encourage or a word spoken that leaves an individual or a church devastated.

The second time it is mentioned is in **1 Corinthians 12:10** where the gift is associated with the move or manifestation of the Holy Spirit. This means at any special occasion the Holy Spirit can come upon a man or woman and give them a word of knowledge or prophetic utterance for that specific occasion only.

One Sunday night on my first trip to Nigeria, I had just preached in my final service for the day. Suddenly, the spirit of prophecy came upon me. As I began to pray for people, the Holy Spirit began to give me prophetic messages for each one of them. Some people were even joining the prayer line for the second time hoping to hear a better word. This had never happened to me before and I was stunned at the way God chose to work that night. By the time I got back home a few days later that special prophetic unction had lifted from my life, but I did not question God about it.

What I could have done after that night was redefine myself as a prophet because that seemed to be more popular than the preaching of the word. Unfortunately, I've seen too many people do that. They place themselves in a specific office based on a **1 Corinthians 12** manifestation of the Holy Spirit. This is extremism.

The third time the prophetic gift is mentioned, is in **Ephesians 4:11-12** where it is used in preparing God's people for works of service. It is mentioned alongside the gifts of Apostle, Evangelist, Pastor and Teacher. Papa Fabe called this "consultant gifts". In other words, these gifts are purely equipping gifts. Obviously, **Ephesians 4** prophets are skilled in delivering a word from God, but they are also skilled in training others to do the same. In reality, these are the only people who can legitimately call themselves prophets. Everyone else are just ministers who are gifted in prophecy or who prophecy in relation to the Spirit's manifestation.

There are sadly many ministers who call themselves prophets but are not involved in the equipping of the saints for works of service. The Bible is crystal clear on how the gifts are to be used and we should avoid extremism at all costs, because it does nothing than cause harm and ill repute to the body of Christ.

Another gift that has been taken to the extreme is the Apostolic gift. In the last 10 years there has been the resurgence of this title at the expense of the other precious gifts in *Ephesians 4*. I will talk more about the apostolic gift in a later chapter.

It is vital that the church understands the spiritual context of *Ephesians 4:11*. In verse 8 we are told that when He (Christ) ascended on high He led captives in His train and gave gifts to men. In other words, whatever Christ carried, He released to men. Since no single person can fully embody all five gifts, Christ decided that He would bestow His prophetic mantle upon some, His Apostolic mantle upon some, His teaching mantle upon some, His pastoral mantle upon some, and His Evangelistic mantle upon some. Notice the word "some" appearing before every gift in the text. The Bible does not say to some and to others. It just says, "to some". This is important because it means that not everybody in the Kingdom would be gifted this specifically since these are also governmental gifts.

These are not status gifts or even titles. These are specific governmental and equipping offices that some people hold. It's that simple. Notice Paul never called himself Apostle Paul. He always starts a letter by introducing himself as Paul called to be an Apostle by the grace of God. It's not a title, but a function.

God never meant that these offices appear on our business cards or e-mail greetings. Not everyone who calls themselves by one of these titles, actually functions in those offices. But that's another topic for another occasion.
Paul states that in some cases he became all things to all men so that he may win some (*1 Corinthians 9:22*). Adopting a title simply places you under immense pressure and for the rest of your days you will have to live up to a public image of the title.

It's way safer to be called by your first name, which Alfie insisted on everywhere he went.

Chapter two

The power of coffee

As a South African, I cannot boast about the coffee we drink in Cape Town. Most homes settle for any brand of instant coffee which just requires boiling water and a spoon or two of coffee powder as a morning beverage. We are not coffee connoisseurs by a long shot.

One of the things Alfie Fabe introduced me to was good coffee. This had nothing to do with any particular brand, but it had everything to do with what happened when two people engaged each other intentionally around an Americano. This chapter is devoted to the most important principle of Alfie Fabe's life and ministry. It is the one thing that governed everything he did. It is the most important thing he taught his family, his leaders and those he mentored.

In both life and ministry, it is often those crisis experiences that form the pivoting point between an old paradigm and a new; between a local ministry and an international one; between the normal and extraordinary.

In 1994 the CEO of the denomination Alfie belonged to, decided to free the churches from that association. They could decide whether they wanted to stay or leave. Alfie chose to leave and not long after that he incurred a back injury, which landed him in hospital. While in hospital, God gave him one word, 'relationships'. Obviously, this was confusing because like so many ministers he was used to a style of ministry that did not place relationships at the forefront of everything else.

With most denominational churches, Pastors were almost forbidden to have close relationships with the parishioners. It was all about the pastoral duty and nothing more. Pastors had to ignore that inner God given need for friendship and devote themselves totally to the care of their congregation. What most did not realise, was that one could not minister effectively without having compassion for the people and their struggles. The Bible tells us that Jesus the Son of God openly displayed compassion on various occasions.

Matthew 9:36 *When he saw the crowds, he had compassion on them, because they were harassed and helpless, like sheep without a shepherd.*

It is virtually impossible to have true compassion without the release of emotions and the desire to bring comfort and care to the individual. The more one spends time with individuals, the more relationships develop. It was a process that was automatic. In fact, it was godly. One just had to see how Jesus develops his relationships with his disciples to the point that one even called himself "the disciple that Jesus loved".

Once a pastor begins to minister to a family or an individual a bond begins to develop between them. A relationship becomes inevitable, and it is not unbiblical. In fact, our deepest relationships today stem from the ministry and the time we invested in certain people. As much as we tried, there was no way to stop what developed. The difficulty was that not everyone in the congregation enjoyed that same level of relationship with us, because we did not meet them at the same level. The result was that some folk believed we had favourites and became resentful. Some even believed, that as a pastoral couple we were not supposed to have friends inside the congregation. There was no way that we could stop this development because growth, healing and restoration were taking place, while strong relationships were developing. This eventually became one of the reasons why we decided to leave. We just could not walk away from the relationships that developed over time. It was only after our exit that we began to learn the truth about relationships.

"It's all about relationships".
-Alfred Gerald Fabe

It is a well-known medical and scientific fact, that life without significant relationships is not only meaningless but very unhealthy.

James Lynch in his book, **The Broken Heart**, says: *"Most of the people I deal with have at the root of their physical problem the problem of loneliness. They may well be living with someone, or indeed in a busy bustling family atmosphere but they do not know what it is like to experience a close relationship. The lonely are twice as likely to suffer physical problems as those who enjoy a warm relationship with at least one other person"*.

Dr Bernard Steinzor in his book, ***The Healing Partnership*** says, *"The person who feels completely alone and has lost hope of a relationship will become a patient in the wards of a mental hospital or bring their life to an end through suicide".*

My first encounter with Alfie took place when he said to me, "let's go for coffee". This was the first of hundreds of encounters over coffee. God chose a popular South African breakfast restaurant to be the place where we would embark on a journey of friendship. It was the greatest journey of my life and it was not being formed in church nor Bible school or our homes. I soon learned and began to enjoy the power of coffee appointments with my spiritual dad. This will remain one of my most treasured memories.

Proverbs 18:24 says *"A man of many companions may come to ruin but there is a friend who sticks closer than a brother".*

Whenever the church quoted this verse, they always referred to Jesus exclusively being that friend who is closer to us than even our family members. While we know this is true, it does not refer to Jesus only. The Bible makes it known that friendships born out of relationships are tighter than family ties.

"We are not wealthy because of money; we are wealthy because of relationships".
-Alfred Gerald Fabe

One of the most vital principles every minister needs to learn very early, is the power of divine relationships. God sends people into your life for very specific reasons. It has to be clearly understood that they all don't have the same redemptive purpose. In other words, not all relationships are there to make us feel good about ourselves, even though we wish they would. Some relationships have very different agendas and modus operandi.

The purpose of some relationships serves to make us feel uncomfortable and challenged. Every time you are around them God seems to reveal something about yourself that He wants to clean up or remove. Their presence and their words bring you to a state of discomfort and deep conviction to the point that your flesh wants to resent their presence in your life. You try to ignore them for these very reasons, yet they are incredibly valuable people. I had many such friends in my lifetime.

There was a man in my first church whose friendship served that purpose. He would irritate me to no end, yet he was the one God used to deal with my arrogance and pride. I thought he had a problem with me because I was a young charismatic preacher and he was much older than me, yet he loved me probably as much as everyone else did and it took me years to understand that his purpose in my life was quite different than the purpose of my cheerleaders. Even though, I disliked it when he challenged me. He challenged my preaching, my leadership style, and every decision that I made. I believed the ministry would be better without him, but I was dead wrong.

Never despise those relationships in which you are profusely challenged and disciplined. Those people are among your most valuable friends.

There are of course people whose agenda it is to destroy you and undermine your leadership. They seem to be gracious to you at the start, but they end up being hurtful, deceptive, and abusive. Unfortunately, those relationships need to be terminated.

So, how do you know whether a relationship is genuine or not? I offer a few suggestions:

- *When you share the same heart and mind over the things of God.* Unfortunately, there are many Christians whom I know and love with all my heart but who do not share the same passion with me for the things of God. They use particularly good words and terminology and even agree with the things I propose, but our hearts and minds are not on the same wave-length. We do not speak the same language when it comes to evangelism, righteousness and walking in victory.

- *When you are able to share a degree of godly intimacy.* When you can meet over coffee and talk about the real things on your heart, then pray with and encourage each other in the Lord. When you leave the presence of someone feeling broken down, abused, and trampled upon then you probably should not be having those meetings any longer.

- *When your relationship causes you to be fruitful.* Intimacy is an important concept in the Bible, because, wherever it is used, something is always produced. What grows out of your relationships? My relationship with Alfie always led to something being produced. Most times it was a change in my character, but other times it meant a new avenue of ministry. I can safely say that every nation I visited for ministry was birthed out of my coffee dates with my spiritual father.

- *When your relationship becomes transparent it creates an atmosphere for repentance.* As a result, joy is produced and ultimately growth in leadership. There have been countless times in my life that I left a meeting with a friend, with a deep conviction on my heart, which in turn led to repentance for my behaviour and foolishness. I knew this was godly conviction because the end result would always result in great joy and an incredible peace in my heart, knowing that God was doing something powerful in my life.

- *When something gets deposited in your life regardless of the conversation.* This was one of my most notable experiences and the one that still tears me up with emotion. Every time I met with my spiritual father there was something in his spirit that would automatically be transferred into me despite the conversations we were having. Most times those conversations were not deeply spiritual or theological, but when I left, I always felt like he handed me a treasure. Something from his life was being transferred to me. I will talk about this more in a later chapter.

"The Kingdom of God is not supposed to be professional but relational".
-Alfred Gerald Fabe

Relationships can either bless us or harm us because the deeper the relationship, the more vulnerable and transparent we have to become. This often means unmasking oneself and portraying the real person inside with all our insecurities, hurts, secrets, and shortcomings.

Kingdom Ministries International is a relationship based organisation and it was started with this principle at the forefront. Alfie Fabe always spoke about relationships being the main thing and informal structures being the second thing, when starting up a ministry. I remember being asked to serve on the board of elders shortly after joining. Before that I had investigated other organisations with the idea of joining them. I looked at their application forms, their constitution and by-laws, their leadership organograms, their form of church government among other things and learnt much in the process. However, in coming to Kingdom Ministries International, I expected something similar, but all I found was a simple teaching on relationships. Then when joining the board of elders, to my peril, I challenged the non-existence of stringent rules and regulations and joining criteria. Well, over time Alfie cut me down to size. In our regular coffee meetings, he shared the principles of relationships vs institutionalism and over time I began to imbibe the immense value of what he was teaching me. I wanted a professional association with my colleagues and Alfie insisted on a relational one.

Since most of us were at one point of our lives connected to an institutional church, this transformation did not happen overnight. It took years but eventually relationship building became paramount, and breakfast and coffee dates the natural off shoot.

In the year 2000, another movement was launched. Through a series of prophetic utterances at various times, the All Nations Conference was birthed. Alfie had a desire to see representatives of many nations coming together in one place to worship God. What he did not plan for, or perhaps even envisage, was the ensuing movement that would result.

There was one principle that would govern this conference. Yes, you've guessed it. The principle of relationships. The idea was that we would extend an invitation to everyone we knew in the nations to come to Cape Town and be part of this event. The criteria were that no one would stay in a hotel or guest house. Each delegate would stay with a family connected to the conference for up to two weeks, at the expense of their hosts. Well, on paper this was better said than done and everyone who looked at this immediately formed their own opinions about how this would not work.

It has now been 20 years since our first conference and the movement still continues.

What happened at the first conference was nothing short of a miracle. People were asked to volunteer hosting at least one guest at their own expense. Because this was a new concept, there were many unforeseen logistical problems which occurred. These were dealt with as they occurred, and we learnt from them. However, at the end of the conference the testimonies that emerged were mind-blowing. What seemed to be an impossible request turned out to be the turning point for most families. Many received healing and miracles in the lives of their children and other family members. Others received financial breakthroughs. Marriages were restored and relationships healed. Young people were set free from drug addiction, but most of all, the hosts themselves were invited to the homes of their guests and it was fascinating watching people scramble to get their passports so they could travel. All this happened in the hosting homes and I can safely say that more miracles happened in people's homes than at the conference itself.

What was the secret? The power of divine relationships. The professional barrier was broken and through relationships people received from God what they had been praying for. From that time on, Pastors no longer embarked on ministry trips by themselves, but now they were being accompanied by members of their congregation. Oh, what a joy that was. I have had that privilege on numerous occasions, both to host ministers and invite church members to accompany me to the nations. This was one sure way to turn every member into a minister and today I delight myself in doing this.

We did however have a few people from time to time who came to our conference with a professional mentality, expecting to be hosted at a five star hotel with luxury and office bearers. Some even tried to insist on this as a requirement for their invitation and our relationship ended after their first visit.

What are the differences between a relational model and a professional model?

- The relational person focusses on people, the professional person focusses on a product.
- The relational person invests in people, the professional person makes money off people. Much of our teaching on giving and sowing can easily just be professional

motivations with a few scripture verses attached. The difference lies in our intentions.

- Relational persons enter lifelong friendships while professional friendships may only last as long as business agreements.
- The relational model encourages transparency, while the professional model believes that 'familiarity breeds contempt.'
- A relational model develops trust and faithfulness between people while a professional model keeps people feeling sceptical about each other.
- Relational models lead people to growth, productivity, and a deeper relationship with God while a professional model can leave people feeling exploited, manipulated, ripped off and discarded.

The Kingdom of God does not function on professional principles. While I do believe that there has to be a degree of diplomacy and ethical integrity that goes with our gifts and offices, we violate the culture of the Kingdom and miss valuable opportunities with our reluctance to connect to people on a personal level.

Chapter three

"Cast the man out of the demon".
-Alfred Gerald Fabe

Alfie used lots of humour both in the pulpit and in his teaching sessions with his sons. There were times when he needed to allude to the severity of a moral character and the steps needed to correct unrighteous behaviour and one of the ways he did so, was by reversing a common phrase used by Pentecostal ministers when performing deliverance ministry. So instead of saying that the demon needs to be cast out of a man, he would often say, "cast the man out of the demon". Sometimes this needs to be received in the humorous way that it is presented, but there are times when we have to stop and think about the validity of that statement in some cases.

In every biblical case of deliverance, we are told that demons were told to leave the people they had infiltrated and immediately those people were set free. There was the occasion, soon after the mount of transfiguration, when Jesus' disciples tried to cast a demon out of a boy. They were unsuccessful and Jesus had to teach them that those kinds only came out by fasting and prayer. Thereafter, Jesus commanded the demon to leave the boy and it came out immediately. **Mark 9:25-27** This was a difficult case, but the demons listened to the voice of Jesus and obeyed.

Another case in point, was the deliverance of the man who lived in the Gadarenes. He lived among the tombs and mutilated himself with sharp stones. He had a legion of demons living inside him. A Roman legion had 6000 soldiers, which means he had that many demons inside him. This gives one the idea that he didn't possess demons, but the demons possessed him. All his actions were controlled by these demons. The Bible says that Jesus commanded the demons to come out of him. In fact, the Greek tense alludes to the fact that Jesus told them over and over again to leave the man (**Mark 5:8**) but they didn't. He then spoke to the man who told Him that his name was Legion, because they were many demons inside him. The demons then begged Jesus over and over again not to send them out of the area. He gave them permission and they came out of the man and went into the pigs. The pigs in turn ran over a cliff and drowned. Obviously, those looking after the pigs went and reported this in the town and country, and everyone went to see what had happened.

By the time they got to Jesus and the place where this man was last seen, they found him fully dressed and in his right mind. This man wanted to accompany Jesus wherever He went, but Jesus gave him a different assignment. Jesus told him to go back to his family and to tell them what the Lord had done for him. This man went away and not only told his family, but he also went to the ten cities of the Decapolis spreading the good news of what Jesus had done for him. The only thing he was armed with was his testimony, but with that, he left the area of his torment and possessions and followed Jesus' command in obedience.

Now allow me to try and place this story in my context.

One of the turning points in my decision to leave my denomination came with a startling prophetic word. On a particular Sunday evening, I was looking forward to a Pastors meeting arranged by some colleagues, but I did not have any money for that event. The Lord promised me that before the night was over He would supply that need. Well at 11.55 that evening as I was just about to retire to bed, someone knocked at my door and upon opening the door the person on the other side said, "the Lord told me a few moments ago to come and give you this". He placed some money in my hand and left immediately without saying anything further. It was just enough money for me to attend the event the next day. Well, that morning at this meeting the Lord began dealing with me. I joined the prayer line and when it was time for me to be ministered to, someone gave me a sharp prophetic utterance. One of the things he said to me was that there was a noose around my neck that was set to destroy me, and that deliverance would come as I surrendered that noose. For the life of me I did not understand what this meant. I thought that it had something to do with the church I was pastoring at the time, but it was not.

A few weeks later I hosted our regional ministers fraternal in my home and one of the men who hosted that eventful Pastors meeting just happened to be the speaker. Well, as he prayed for me, he pointed to my graduation picture on display on one of the cupboards. "That's the noose" he said. "It's your graduation hood". Now I was even more confused, because I had studied for 4 years to earn my degree that qualified me to gain ministerial recognition with that denomination. The truth is, as a graduate I had become very dogmatic about the things I believed, and I never allowed the Holy Spirit the freedom to do anything. It was either the way of my dogma or no way. I began to realise that it was time to lay my theology down and allow the Holy Spirit to take full control of my life. I used to believe in the Father, Son and Holy Scriptures and excluded the Holy Spirit. My ministry had thus become clinical and predictive. God then started me on a journey of discovering who He was, all over again, and what a ride that was, and still is.

As a Baptist minister, I majored on minors and left out the most important ingredient to life and ministry, the Holy Spirit.

When I laid down my qualifications at the feet of Jesus it felt as if I was stepping out of a graveyard and into a place of power and authority. My qualifications became my place of bondage and I needed to be freed from it.
There are times when ministers have to make the choice of laying down good things so they can walk in better things.   The most liberating thing in life is the knowledge that we are sons of God, which means that we do not have to live up to the expectations that our qualifications or titles deserve.

Galatians 5:1 *It is for freedom that Christ has set us free. Stand firm then, and do not let yourselves be burdened again by a yoke of slavery.*

"Don't turn a tissue into an issue".
-Alfred Gerald Fabe

Alfie Fabe often made this statement with his dry sense of humour, but how I wish more ministers would hear this over and over again, especially in the year 2020. We have become experts in taking small insignificant things and turning them into huge problems. We specialize in turning molehills into mountains.

In the mid 1990's, my wife and I spent lots of time in deliverance ministry. It was not an extremely popular thing at the time and one of the problems church leaders made was to see demonic problems where there were none.

One night the elders of a Pentecostal church called us to the home of a leader whose teenage daughter was reported to be possessed by demons. Because it was a family situation, I decided to take my parents along. We started talking to the girl, who had once given her life to Christ, and her parents, and we soon realised that the symptoms they were describing had nothing to do with demons. In fact, the girl (being a typical teenager) had simply missed out on prayer meetings and a few services which led the elders to diagnose a demonic problem. This girl was never taught about the assurance of salvation and her position in Christ. All she knew was a form of religion that guaranteed her salvation through works. As we started sharing these things with her, it was as if a floodlight had been switched on in her life. She needed her mind renewed. She did not need to be set free from demons.
Guess who needed the real deliverance, yes, her parents and the church leaders. So many leaders need this type of deliverance.

Notice how Paul described his deliverance ministry in
2 Corinthians 10:4-5. *[4]The weapons we fight with are not the weapons of the world. On the contrary, they have divine power to demolish strongholds. [5]We demolish arguments and every pretension that sets itself up against the knowledge of God, and we take captive every thought to make it obedient to Christ.*

The greatest strongholds in life are the ones in our minds. Those belief systems, paradigms, religious perspectives and old wife's tales that if not dealt with eventually end up governing our belief systems and affecting the way we exercise faith. The truth is that many of these things are not even blatant heresies but niggling "issues" that can hinder our relationship with God.

I have observed the same attitude on social media and my heart breaks into many pieces at the judgements Christians pass at leaders. The modern church unfortunately has many Pharisees. In fact, it seems that Jesus did not have to deal with as many Pharisees as we have to deal with today. It is one of the stains upon the modern church. Everyone has a judgement to pass based on their interpretation of scripture and some of the leaders under judgement also happen to be some of the godliest men and women on the planet today. I guess it has become easy to pass judgement on one end of the telephone or computer screen without having to challenge your opponent face to face.

There are basic things that should unite us not divide us.
The death of Jesus on the cross as a vicarious sacrifice for all mankind through which sinful man is redeemed back to God.
Salvation and peace with God only come through repentance and receiving the gift of eternal life, by faith in the finished work of the cross.

Baptism and the Lord's supper become elements through which we celebrate the finished work of the cross. The Holy Spirit indwells every believer at conversion and leads him into a relationship with God. In whose name we baptise believers, what we believe about the gifts of the spirit and speaking in tongues, how we worship, etc, are things not vital to salvation and by castigating one another over these things we are doing nothing other than bringing shame to the kingdom of God.

Notice what Paul said in *1 Corinthians 2:1-2* *¹And so it was with me, brothers, and sisters. When I came to you, I did not come with eloquence or human wisdom as I proclaimed to you the testimony about God. ²For I resolved to know nothing while I was with you except Jesus Christ and Him crucified.*

This leads me to my next point.

> *"Salvation is about Faith in Christ plus nothing".*
>
> -Alfred Gerald Fabe

From time to time people came into our fellowship and they would propagate a theology of works that accompany faith in Christ in order to obtain salvation. Let me explain what I mean.

Some years ago, a dear brother visited Kingdom Ministries International and almost immediately began to spread a doctrine called, "Circumcision of the Heart" or "The cutting of the flesh" as Paul speaks about in *Colossians 2:9-12* *⁹For in Christ all the fullness of the Deity lives in bodily form, ¹⁰and in Christ you have been brought to fullness. He is the head over every power and authority. ¹¹In Him you were also circumcised with a circumcision not performed by human hands. Your whole self-ruled by the flesh was put off when you were circumcised by Christ, ¹²having been buried with Him in baptism, in which you were also raised with Him through your faith in the working of God, who raised Him from the dead.*

This teaching made one believe that you were not walking in freedom unless you went through a ritual in which the heart was circumcised. In line with **verse 12**, it was taught that the ritual to circumcise the heart had to be baptism, regardless of one's previous baptism as a believer. In other words, unless one experienced a circumcision of your heart at believer's baptism, that baptism was invalid.

So, this brother went about recruiting followers and even though this sounded good and godly it was contrary to what the Bible actually taught. This doctrine simply added this ritual as part of the conversion experience.

Here's what I have experienced with strange doctrines. They normally get introduced to Christians who are hungry for a new move of God in their lives. Somehow the enemy knows what you desire. He is not omniscient, but he monitors your conversations and your prayer life and become privy to the things you speak to God about. And so, in relation to what you ask, he will introduce someone into your life to lead you astray. That is why we need to stay in relationship with people who are wise and seasoned. If a doctrine is off, they will know.

Alfie Fabe reacted to this very strongly and one of the things he vigorously taught until he died was that Salvation is by faith in Christ alone, plus nothing. Every time we add an extra ingredient or practice to the exercise of repentance and faith at conversion, we begin to sow deception and a false gospel.

Now a closer look at the Colossians passage will tell us that fullness in Christ and the circumcision of the flesh has already happened at conversion. Notice the tense. Paul is not telling the church to please circumcise their hearts. He is simply telling them that their hearts have already been circumcised at conversion. He did not teach a baptism of circumcision of hearts. The baptism taught in the New Testament is the Baptism that demonstrates outwardly what Christ has already done inwardly. We have been buried with Him and we rose to new life in Him. This is a testimony to the world of the great work of grace accomplished in our lives.

Paul dealt with this type of thing in Galatians when some Judaizers entered the city of Galatia (a Gentile city) and like the strategy of modern day Jehovah witnesses they said to the people: "we are so glad that you are saved, but in order to retain your salvation you also have to be circumcised". Paul rebukes the Galatians sharply for allowing themselves to be deceived by these cunning individuals.

Galatians 3:1-4 [1]You foolish Galatians! Who has bewitched you? Before your very eyes Jesus Christ was clearly portrayed as crucified. [2]I would like to learn just one thing from you: Did you receive the Spirit by the works of the law, or by believing what you heard? [3]Are you so foolish? After beginning by means of the Spirit, are you now trying to finish by means of the flesh? [4]Have you experienced so much in vain—if it really was in vain?

There is a popular Christian magazine in America that has been hosting articles relating to the Christian electoral position in the 2020 presidential election. From time to time there were articles openly stating that voters could not call themselves Christians while they voted for a certain political party or presidential candidate. This is not a joke.

The obvious problem with the authors of these articles was that they were propagating a political position as a requirement for salvation. I have read similar articles saying the same things from the political standpoint of both major parties. (My purpose is not to shame any person or organisation, so I refrain from using personal or organisational names in such cases.) This is as close as one gets to heresy. This is a blatant and calculated twisting of Biblical truth. We need to beware of such people.

Proverbs 4:23 says: *"Above all else, guard your heart, for everything you do flows from it".*

If you allow heresy to infiltrate your heart you will be teaching that same heresy very soon and according to the Bible you will be held accountable for the things you teach.
This leads me to the next thing Alfie said.

"A failure is someone who cannot accept God's plan of Salvation".
-Alfred Gerald Fabe

If you are considering serving in Christian ministry as a lay leader or holding a five-fold ministry office, then you have to understand that throughout your ministry you will fail. You will fail every day for the rest of your life. Now that's not a very encouraging thing to say to young aspiring men and women of God. No matter how much you have studied and trained for your position you are destined to fail more times than you succeed.

Failure is something that most people have a problem dealing with, but please do yourself a huge favour. Go to the person you consider to be your mentor in ministry and ask them some questions like:

a) Have you ever failed in ministry?
b) How many times have you failed in your years of ministry?
c) How often have you failed at a task and had to repeat that task or make reparation?
d) You may even ask, have you had a moral failure?
e) How do you see yourself after failing so many times?

These are important questions because they often determine whether people stay in ministry or not.

Now, everyone I know in ministry, especially me, have all failed in ministry more times than we wish to remember. We have all been down the road of beating and condemning ourselves. That is normal too. But what made some of us remain in ministry is how we saw ourselves when all was said and done.

There were some who simply just decided to hang up their gloves because they began to see themselves as failures. They simply were not prepared to risk more possible failures and endure further humiliation. The ministry had become too painful. What I have realised in life is that sometimes the problem does not really lie with the mistakes we make, but with how we see ourselves in the light of God's plan of salvation.

In our counseling ministry with couples, Anne and I have very often encountered individuals or couples who had just given up on life. They had made too many mistakes in life and ministry and were about to throw in the towel. In trying to help them

find a way through their pain, one of the simple exercises Anne does is to hand them a list of scripture verses that they have to read for themselves. As they read those verses, they have to add their name or personal pronoun in the subject.
e.g. I am accepted in the beloved (**Ephesians 1:6**), I am fearfully and wonderfully made (**Psalm 139:14**) He keeps me from falling (**Jude 1:24**) etc.

They are then to transfer those verses onto cards and stick them in the places in their homes they frequent the most, e.g., on the bathroom mirror or refrigerator door. Every time they stand in those places, they are to verbally repeat those verses over and over again.

A sure way to deal with these feelings of failure is to daily lay claim to the salvation plan of God in your life by repeating who you are in Him, because of what Jesus did on the cross.
Someone once said that *"a failure is not someone who falls down, but someone who fails to get up once he has fallen"*.
Do not allow your failures to determine who you are.
Remember you were God's idea and when He had a specific mission, He thought of you first. He chose you to finish what He gave you to do. So, do what successful people do every day. Speak to yourself. Preach to yourself. Leaders know how to encourage themselves in the Lord.

"Eat the meat and spit out the bones".

-Alfred Gerald Fabe

Another one of Alfie Fabe's common phrases was the above one, but it comes with an important principle. There is no

person on the planet that can lay claim to possessing ultimate truth. Even though we have amazing teachers sharing the word of life, no one can claim to have ultimate truth. All of the preachers I love listening to have an area in their theology that I don't agree with. Does it mean they are false teachers? Of course not. Some of their teaching on certain subjects is just off but they are brilliant, sharp, and anointed on other issues.
Even our spiritual father didn't claim to possess all truth and so he always would tell his sons, whenever I preach, eat the meat, and spit out the bones. In other words, receive and digest the things that feed our spirit and discard the rest. If it doesn't feed your spirit you don't have to have nightmares because of it, unless of cause, it brings you to a point of conviction of sin. In that case repent and move on.

Now, as a minister you need to understand that people will do the very same with the things you say. The Lord has taught me a long time ago, not to be offended when people do not respond favourably to every part of my sermon. I understand that not every part of my sermon is supposed to feed everyone. People will take what they need and discard the rest. I simply need to go back to the Holy Spirit and check with Him if I had been telling the truth. Does this mean that I have to stop sharing the gospel or teaching? Absolutely not. As we grow in the grace and gift of teaching, we learn to refine that gift and to depend on the Holy Spirit to lead us into all truth.

"Don't be afraid of change because change brings growth".

-Alfred Gerald Fabe

This next bit is the battle ground and probably graveyard for many leaders as it has to do with something we all have a love/hate relationship with. It is change. Change will either make you or break you. Many people have given up because of change. In fact, most leaders despise change. Now, it is true that some folks are not wired to welcome change all the time. They love the familiar, the routine of a predictable program, but for goodness' sake don't you dare change that and all hell breaks loose.

We all know that according to the Bible, God does not change. He is the same yesterday, today and forever, according to **Hebrews 13:8.**

Malachi 3:6 says: *"I the Lord do not change".*

However, we need to understand that this has nothing to do with what God does, but with who He is. His moral Character does not change. As He was yesterday, He will be today. Also, His promises do not change. God never goes back on His word.

Psalm 119:89 says: *"Your word O Lord is eternal it stands firm in the heavens".*

But as we read the scriptures, especially the way God deals with leaders, we are confronted with the fact that nowhere in all of scripture do we find God doing the same thing twice. We always find Him doing a different thing with a different leader. Now, His divine purposes are not violated, He just decides to use a different method to get us there, and He does this consistently throughout the Bible. No two leaders have the same experience with God. This speaks to our uniqueness in His sight.

Change comes in all shapes and forms.

Sometimes God speaks to us and tells us to change a few things in our lives or ministry. This is one of the gentle ways in which He institutes change.

For some of us, transitioning to new technology can be a challenge. In the late 1980's and 1990's, leaders were faced with the new challenge of transitioning to computers. It was a challenge for those of us who could not type. Only girls took typing classes at school, boys did technology and woodwork and so when the time came to transition, the baby-boomer generation of males struggled immensely.
Many were not ready to change with the times and even today some still use pen and paper for their sermon notes.

Change can also occur in times of crisis or sickness.

I mentioned earlier how God spoke to Alfie while he was in hospital with a back injury and that crisis moment led him to make the most important transition of his ministry.
Crisis moments or seasons are usually pivotal in bringing change.

On December 31, 2019, my wife and I were sitting in Gdansk airport on our way home from a short break away. We had lots of time to kill, so in between dinner and boarding our flight we checked our social media accounts and true to form on the last day of the year, best wishes for the coming year were beginning to roll in. All kinds of prophetic declarations were being made and appropriate scripture verses were circulating. Many folks were talking about 2020 being the year in which we would draw near to God. The evening news was on one of the television screens and amid the scrolling we briefly glanced at the clips. There was a report out of China about a virus, that apparently had started in a market and was now beginning to spread all over the province. Now, this was not the first time we watched a news report about a flu like virus. There were many viruses that emerged from the east like SARS, bird flu, swine flu etc, but had dissipated within a short time. We had no idea that within eight months, we would have lost 3 family members, our spiritual father and a large number of friends and colleagues to this virus, that was set to ravage the globe. We spent our summer vacation this year watching funerals on social media at the rate of two to three per week. It was a season we did not plan nor prepare for.

As this virus morphed from a local viral infection to an epidemic and then a pandemic, we saw the world change within a few months. Countries were locking down communities in an effort to stem the flow of this virus. Social distancing became the new practise and masks became the new uniform. The corporate and secular world quickly adapted to this new phenomenon, but alas the church struggled, and we are still struggling.

Three months into the epidemic God spoke to me and clearly said, don't expect church to be the same again.
In the meantime, ministers were practising social disobedience, exercising their constitutional amendment rights, and going crazy and very few decided to consult with God concerning His next move. Change has come through an incredibly sad and sorrowful season.

There will come times in our lives that God will bring us to the precipice of change, through trouble, pain and even loss, and despite the circumstances, we will have to make the decision to change. The decision is always ours to make. In those moments we must always remember that change always brings growth. We cannot be doing the same thing over and over again expecting a new result. If we desire growth, we have to make the change.

I am always reminded of the events in the early church, after the death of Stephen in *Acts 7*. The first verse of the next *chapter (8:1)* tells us that a great persecution broke out in Jerusalem, which resulted in the scattering of the church all over the province of Judea and Asia Minor. People believed that this event was the end of the church, but the opposite was the case. Everywhere they went they duplicated themselves by making disciples and starting house churches. The result was that in a very short time, the gospel had spread throughout the ungodly Asia Minor. Change precipitated growth.

This may be the scariest season of your life, but it is important that you allow the Holy Spirit to lead you towards your greatest victory. Our experience has always been, the greater the pain and loss, the greater the victory that lies ahead. There is great victory ahead. Pursuing it will not be what we are used to, but seasons do change, and we will yet see the greatest harvest of souls this world has ever seen.

Chapter four

Fathers and sons

Dr Seuss said: *"Be who you are and say what you feel because those who mind don't matter and those who matter don't mind".*

As a South African living In Iceland, I often reflect on my heritage and the history of my people, yet when I do, much of those memories are not filled with nostalgia, but with sadness and regret. Because, as in the case of people who have their roots in slavery, we don't know who we are. My beloved people have a problem identifying themselves. In Cape Town, we are known as *"coloured"* people or mixed race (a derogatory term implying that we are bastards). Many of us have traced our roots back to the first nation people of South Africa called the Koi-Koi or San people, but sadly there are very few historical records available today. The rest of us have the blood of many nations flowing through our veins, because of the hideous things our ancestral mothers had to endure at the hands of their colonial slave masters.

Apartheid placed us on a lower rank than European fair skinned, blue eyed people, to the extent that we once believed and even repeated the narrative that we would never be good enough.

When Apartheid was finally abolished and a new democratic government established, we believed that things would finally change for us. But even though huge politically changes occurred, not much has changed for us.

- We still make the same statements concerning our lack of resources.
- We still look at people of other races with suspicion and disdain.
- We don't allow others to prosper in life without casting suspicion on how they got there.
- We still remain crippled with insecurity.

Extremely little has been done to rid ourselves of the mentality of the past. Now, imagine having someone like that as your pastor. He may be greatly anointed by the Lord for a specific ministry. He may also be gifted to do what he does. He may excel at preaching and prophesying, and his ministry may even yield fruit, but what he does behind the scenes, when interacting with other individuals, depends on how he sees himself.

This next statement I make with the utmost respect towards my colleagues, but here's the issue. My heart bleeds over the fact that the only people who want to be known by their ecclesiastical titles are those who have come through a lineage of slavery or colonialism.

When we first visited Iceland in 2004, we discovered that no one in Iceland was addressed according to their title. Ministers, doctors, magistrates are called by their first names, even the president, yet there is no sense of insecurity.

When Papa Fabe visited Iceland in 2011 and 2017, wherever he preached he was always introduced as Alfie Fabe, not pastor or apostle, and guess what, he absolutely loved it. I remember when pastoring my first church, I thought that my title brought me respect and I always introduced myself as Pastor Ron. Well, this had a negative spin off for me and it was a defining moment in my life, when one of my colleagues heard my son call me 'Pastor' one day and he sharply rebuked me.

After meeting Alfie, I made an amazing discovery, which changed everything for me. Alfie began to talk to me about the fact that the only title the New Testament places on me is the title *"son"*.

Galatians 3:26 calls us sons. Listen to this. *"You are all sons of God through faith in Christ Jesus"* (NIV). *"By faith in Christ you are in direct relationship with God"*. (MSG)

I studied ***Galatians 3:26 – 4:7*** for a while and during that time I felt like my mindset was being removed and a new identity was being implanted. Now, my new identity was there since the day of my conversion, but I had never walked in the fullness of all that the passage implied. I was a son but still living, functioning, and ministering as a slave.

Many people allude to having a spiritual father in their lives but still live as slaves because they don't know the joy of walking in a father-son relationship with God. Your true identity is that of a son.

Some translations of the verse use the phrase "children of God". The Greek specifically uses the word "son". In fact, it is gender specific. This was important in the Jewish context. Does the word exclude females? Absolutely not. Females are included in the term "son" and the reason they are included is because God wanted no gender distinction when it came to inheritance or functionality.

Sons in a Jewish household were heirs (daughters were heirs by virtue of marriage) and they were given specific responsibilities. They carried out their fathers bidding. They represented their fathers in the marketplace. The weight of the business was eventually placed on their shoulders.

According to this passage however, we have all been given the right of inheritance alongside our big brother, Jesus. We have also been given divine impartation to carry out whatever our Father's desire is, whether male or female.

As I studied this passage intently, I sensed God telling me that I never have to go by a title any longer, because the greatest title has been inferred on me. From that day on I have learnt to be secure in the knowledge that I belong to Him and He belongs to me.

I pray that as you read this you may be cleansed from all

insecurities that may have governed your ministry, and that you may find your place in Him as a son. You are a son of God before you are anything else. Here's the test. Will you feel disrespected if a child calls you by your first name and not your title? If so, I encourage you to allow the Holy Spirit to cleanse your soul so you can begin to function as a true son. It is only when we function as sons of God that the next dimension of sonship can become a reality.

Man is a 'tri-partheid' being. He is body, soul, and spirit. Man is essentially spirit; he possesses a soul and lives in a body. It is with our spirits that we relate to God. It is on that level that our sonship is first and foremost established. Things must happen spiritually first before they can happen naturally.

The next dimension of sonship is being in relationship with someone who becomes our father in the faith. In many cases, this is the person who led us to the Lord and then walked us through life. They model Christ in front of us and disciple us to become like Christ. These people also walk us through ministry, and this should be a permanent relationship. Like biological fathers, they show us how things ought to be done, then they do it with us before allowing us to do it on our own. Once I understand sonship through my relationship with God this bit becomes easy.

My relationship with Alfie has taught me how vital this relationship is for every minister.

"Every minister must identify his/her spiritual father".

-Alfred Gerald Fabe

This I believe is an important step for anyone who wishes to make an impact in the nations today.

In the above paragraph I said that in many cases the person who led us to faith in Christ, who disciples us in life and mentors us in ministry is our spiritual father. I use the term spiritual father to differentiate between a natural father and a father in the Lord.

There are however cases where a spiritual father is not the one who led us to the Lord. In my case I was in ministry for a number of years before I realised how vital this was, and because Alfie began to play that role in my life, I adopted him as my "spiritual father". This was not difficult. He did not take the place of God in my life. In fact, he always pointed me to the Lord.

1 Corinthians 4:15 Paul said to the Christians at Corinth *"Even if you had ten thousand guardians in Christ, you do not have many fathers, for in Christ Jesus I became your father through the gospel".*

It is clear that many of these Christians came to faith in Christ through Paul's ministry, but Paul did not stay in Corinth for long. In fact, he visited the city on more than one occasion and between visits many others came to faith in Christ.

Paul became their father in the gospel too, because he loved them, nurtured them, and discipled them. If you are starting out in ministry today and lack a spiritual father, then my advice is that you prayerfully find one that will walk with you, disciple you and mentor you.

"When you don't have a spiritual father, you are an orphan and there are many orphans today".

-Alfred Gerald Fabe

This is a very serious statement that doesn't address our lack as much as it addresses our character.

What do I mean?

It is easy to identify someone who has a spiritual father.

We were ministering in Nigeria for the first time and halfway through our visit we were introduced to a respected man of God. He had just moved house that day and was exhausted. He graciously welcomed us into his new home for a visit that was supposed to be brief. Well, we left his house nearly four hours later. After meeting him we started chatting and suddenly the Holy Spirit fell upon us. We started praying and prophesying and that lasted for about three hours. At the end of that period, he made a startling statement: "I would like to meet your father in the Lord". He discerned our hearts, which led him to identify the spirit of sonship. The following year we introduced him to Alfie and they immediately bonded. It was supernatural. Today we share a wonderful partnership in the gospel as spiritual sons of Alfie Fabe.

There are unfortunately many spiritual orphans in the kingdom today. How do we know this?

- **These leaders are not accountable to anybody.** They have become a law unto themselves. They do things with impunity and do not accept discipline from anybody. So much abuse takes place today, because leaders are not in relationship with someone who can walk them through character issues. Because everybody has a camera phone, much of the horrific things that leaders do are recorded and placed on social media. Everyone pokes fun at them, and some want to beat them up, but they are simply viewing the actions of orphans. Their characters have not been refined through a father/son relationship.

- **They teach heresy.** I'm not talking about slight doctrinal differences; I'm talking about teachings contrary to the Word of God. Doctrines of demons. Here's the litmus test: If your teaching fails to lead people into a relationship with Jesus, becoming fully dependant on Him in all matters of faith and practise, where your influence in their life begins to fade as that happens, then you may very well be teaching heresy. Heresy does not have to be a different doctrine. It may be dressed up in all kinds of Christian clichés and even contain tons of proof texts, but if the purpose is to glorify you and not Christ then it is heresy. We constantly need to check our teaching motives prayerfully.

- **They are power mongers.** They always jostle for position and they crave recognition. These are people who always want to hang out with the senior leaders. They invite them for dinners, take them on holiday, buy them expensive gifts and it's not out of honour or respect but it's because they want something in return. They want power. Be extremely careful when walking with such folk. They don't need power, they need fathering. I will deal with fathering in the next chapter. There is nothing safer and more fulfilling than walking with a spiritual father and then at the appropriate time having him/her release you into a position of leadership. By the time they do this, your character would have had some refinement and your ulterior motivation for leadership would have been replaced by that of a true servant to the body of Christ.

"There is a difference between sons and slaves".

-Alfred Gerald Fabe

Spiritual slavery is closely tied to orphanhood. The difference is that, in most cases, orphans do not walk in relationship with any senior leader. They are lone rangers. Slaves, on the other hand, may be part of the ministry. They may even be friends with the leader, yet they remain slaves. The difference lies in their motives.

Here are some differences between sons and slaves.

1. Slaves live and work in the house while sons build the house. A slave does what he is told to do because, at the end of the day, he is remunerated by the slave master. He is not interested in anything else other than what he has been instructed to do. His only motivation is his remuneration. He wants the money.
   Luke 15:11-31 is a parable about a father and two sons. Now, without deviating from the singular meaning of the parable, one cannot ignore the Jewish context that it addresses without learning some valuable lessons from it. The younger son wanted his inheritance prematurely and because he had not matured suffi-ciently, he asked for it and then went off and spent it wildly. When he reached rock bottom, he realised that the servants in his father's household were living better than he was, and he decided to go back home, not as a son, but as a hired servant, which was indeed how he approached his father. He was a son biologically, but a slave spiritually.

Slaves are those who are only in ministry for what they can derive from it. Sons, on the other hand, are those who are ready to place their ministry ideals on hold for the sake of building the vision of their father. Sons embrace their father's vision as make it their own. This is important.

2. Another difference between sons and slaves lies in who they relate to. If you are in submission to a control freak then the chances are that you are not a son but a slave,

because all you have been doing was keep him/her happy. They have not spent time investing into your life. They have not taken time to explore your gifts with the purpose of raising you up as a minister. Control freaks are extremely insecure people. They will not allow you to excel in your gifting lest you become a threat to them and gain the favour of the people. Many years ago, I did a short term asset management assignment with a company. My immediate superior happened to be a Christian and quite a gifted one at that, but his job in his church was that of a parking attendant, which he did for years. I asked him if he had ever been given something else to do or earmarked for leadership mentoring, and he told me no. He was a gifted leader in the marketplace and a slave in his church.

In his book *"Where are the Fathers"* Alfie Fabe succinctly gives some more differences, which I wish to delineate at this point.

- **Sons are protecting the family while slaves raise the issues.** A true son makes sure no harm or dishonour comes to the family, whereas a slave will always raise issues regardless of the harm they cause. Slaves love church politics, because through it, they can score points with either the leaders or the people.
- **Sons take ownership when things go wrong.** They humble themselves and seek to make restitution. Slaves apportion blame and then stand back and enjoy the fallout.
- **Sons cover the nakedness of their father.** Slaves however are eager to expose their leader to shame and

destruction. By "nakedness" I'm not referring to sin, but weakness. All leaders have weaknesses. We have not yet been glorified, we still live in a mortal body and a sinful world. We still get sick, angry, frustrated, and weary. A true son knows when his father is naked and covers him. When I served KMI as director my late natural father who had been leading one of our churches suffered a mild stroke. As a result, he suffered memory lapses and very often this would manifest in the pulpit. The people started to talk about it, and some made fun of him. As soon as I heard about it, I called him aside and told him as lovingly as I could that I needed him to be my dad and confidant for a very long time and that I wished to relieve him of the burden of the ministry. I did not bring up the issue, I covered his nakedness because I knew he was vulnerable in that area. He then served as an advisor to his successor and as part of the board of KMI for a few years before stepping down with dignity.

- **Sons do not leave their fathers.** When you read the story of Elijah and his son Elisha in *2 **Kings** 2* you will notice how, despite being requested by Elijah to stay in the cities they visited, Elisha did not want to leave his side. This happened three times and every time Elisha gave him the same answer. I will never leave your side. He stuck to his father like glue. There is something to be said about sons who stay by the side of their fathers through thick and thin. They are usually the ones who inherit. If you wish to inherit what your father has, then the secret is to be ready to stay with him through the muddy ground and the stormy weather. When your reputation doesn't matter anymore then you are ready to inherit what your father has. When things get difficult in ministry slaves will resign and look for a better church.

- **Sons do not seek wealth they seek impartation.** I'm not sure what Elijah owned but whatever it was, Elisha did not want it. He was after an impartation. He asked for a double portion of Elijah's spirit. Slaves will go after the physical things.

- **Finally, only true sons will become true fathers.** Slaves may become CEOs and even Pastors and carry fancy titles, but they will never raise sons, because they have not been fathered.

"The most effective tool to disciple the entire church is the father son order".

-Alfred Gerald Fabe

Large amounts of books have been written on the subject of discipleship. In fact, there are organisations around the world right now whose sole purpose is to facilitate discipleship. There is a huge focus on growing Christians into the stature of Christ and that is honourable. I indeed applaud these leaders for the work they do.

One of the huge challenges we face in Iceland is a discipleship one. Hardly any discipleship is done in the evangelical churches here. People are led to Christ and then left to fend for themselves. Imagine telling a baby on the day he is born:

"Welcome into our home, we hope you will have a good and happy life here. We will show you around the house so you can get acquainted with stuff. Here is the bathroom where you clean yourself, the kitchen where you can fix all your meals, your special room where you sleep every night. If you have any questions, then please feel free to ask us". That sounds absurd, but that is what many churches do. People are led to Christ but then are left to fend for themselves.

We focus all our energy on things God never told us to do and very little or no energy on the things he did tell us to do. As far as I know, the job of regeneration is purely the Holy Spirit's. He alone can take a scoundrel and turn him into a loving son. He alone can deal with the sting and effects of sin. We cannot. In reality, we should not be taking credit for people coming into the kingdom. Our initial job is to preach the gospel and leave the results to God. But it doesn't stop there. We are commanded over and over again in scripture to make disciples of all nations.

It's like fishing. We throw the bait; God puts the fish on the hook and then we clean it. It's that simple, yet one of the main problems with maturity in the body of Christ is, we have fish that have not been cleaned. Some of them lead our worship sessions, others lead our youth ministry and I have met some in pastoral leadership. Christians need discipleship.

I have always marvelled at the Pentecostal churches in Cape Town. When I was a young Christian, these churches did not have the facilities that many of our established churches had. Their strategy was simple. They would conduct a meeting in your house and as you give your life to Christ, they recruit you immediately. That week they spend time with you. Then you accompany them to the next meeting, where you now see how things are done. The leaders model their lifestyle in front of you all the time and before long you begin to imitate them. At the same time, they start preparing you to share your testimony and within a few short weeks you share your testimony in one of those meetings. Irrespective of how you sound or the words you use, their response and cheering overwhelm you and you desire to share it over and over again.

People who are acquainted with your past life are amazed and comment about the change that has come over you. Within six months of your conversion, you are preaching a simple gospel message in their meetings.

These folks don't leave you alone until you are ready to lead your own group of people doing what they taught you to do. There was no formal church discipleship program held in class-room format to make you astute in the scriptures, but you were discipled.

Discipleship has never been meant to be conducted in a classroom. Jesus discipled the twelve on the go. He modelled righteousness while at the same time involving them in everything he did. What an amazing model. That is indeed why the father-son order is the best way to disciple the entire church.

In the next chapter I will expand this concept.

Chapter five

Confident fathering

The last 23 years have made me realise that the greatest lack in the world today is not food or water or resources, even though we would like to believe it. It is the lack that plagues poor communities in almost every nation of the world. It is the single deficiency in the lives of 95 percent of incarcerated males. It is the reason why girls make huge mistakes when choosing their life partner.

It is the reason why we have an abundance of males but very few men.

"An individual is a male from the waist down but a man from the shoulders up."
-Anonymous

It features high on the list of contributing factors with regards to women and child abuse, male suicide, violent crimes, academic dropouts, and bad health.

Yes, you've guessed it. It is father deprivation. There is a lack of fathers in nearly every society on the planet.

This problem manifests in two ways:

- **Absent fathers**. Children are raised by single moms. Fathers are non-resident.
- **Immature dads**. These are men who live with their families, but they have checked out as fathers or they just lack the skills to father a family.

This problem manifests itself in the kingdom as well, and even though there is a difference of opinion about the need for fathers, a closer look into the life of an individual quickly reveals a deprivation in the areas of discipling, mentoring, training, and discipline. So, as a result we have a generation of spiritual boys entering ministry who are insecure, obnoxious, arrogant, and proud. This leads to great abuses in the church today.

Alfie Fabe was a father per excellence, who fathered both his biological and spiritual families with the utmost care of a father. In the latter part of his life, he made a statement that should ring true for every father. *"I retired from leadership but not from parenting"*.

Alfie believed that every minister should be a father or become a father. If your fathering skills are not good, then it is necessary to attach yourself to a father and be fathered.

In my early years of ministry, I was failing as a father. I may have been a good preacher, but my fathering skills left much to be desired. When I met Alfie, things began to change for me. The power of the Holy Spirit started to chip away at my insecurities and character flaws, as Alfie through his lifestyle began to impart some important virtues.

As I start this discussion, I wish to present some basic principles of spiritual fathering.

- **Good fathers know how to raise their sons.** There is a belief that someone can only be a spiritual son if you *"begat"* them. Well, firstly when someone comes to Christ then God first and foremost becomes their Father regardless of who led them to Christ. That is settled in scripture.
  Galatians 3:26 *You are all sons of God through faith in Christ Jesus.*

So, no one can occupy that ultimate and eternal role of Father, other than God. What I do believe is that God equips certain leaders with the skills to raise sons for himself. There is a fascinating verse in **Exodus 2:9** after Moses was found in the basket among the reeds by Pharaoh's daughter. His sister said to her, "shall I go and find someone to nurse him for you?" Well, she came back with his mother and Pharaoh's daughter said: *"take this baby and nurse him for me and I will pay you"*. This verse would not be in the Bible if there was not a hidden principle conveyed. The principle is that God adopts sons and then He hands them to us for parenting. What about Elijah and Elisha? Elisha was someone else's son. In fact, he left his natural father and attached himself to Elijah who became his spiritual father. Same principle. So, let's put that argument to rest and accept the surrogate role that God has given to his church, the role of raising up sons. When we raise sons, we deposit values and virtues into them. We shape their lives so that they can do what we've been doing.

- **Good fathers do not turn the fatherless away.** This is obvious. If God is our true Father, then no father should turn away a son who needs to be raised. The kingdom of God is filled with men and woman who may belong to big ministries, but who have not been fathered. That's the sad part. They may have been gifted tremendously, but without correct training they will never be able to utilize the gifts and callings in tandem with a good character. The job of a spiritual father is to instil those values that will enhance their gifts.

- **Good fathers know when to release their sons.** There was an important ceremony in Jewish culture which was called the adoption ceremony. This had nothing to do with accepting an orphan but with what happened when the son reached the age of adoption, which was normally around 30 years. When the son turns 30 the father gathers his friends and business partners and introduces the boy to the business world. This is his way of releasing the boy and the phrase that is used is this one, *"this is my beloved son in whom I am well pleased"*. Of course, this was the phrase God used when Jesus was baptised. When He came up out of the water God said, *"this is my beloved son in whom I am well pleased, listen to him"*. What the Jewish father was saying to his friends was that he was now empowering his son to transact on his behalf. That is indeed the goal of fathering. Every son that is raised must be endowed with the ability to transact on behalf of God. Every spiritual father needs to remember this. Your son does not belong to you. If you keep him you turn him into your possession and he becomes your slave, but when you release him at the proper time, he becomes your adopted son. So, adoption has nothing to do with what we receive, it has everything to do with what we release.

- **Good fathers always seek to restore erring sons.** Someone said, there are only two definite things in life; death, and taxes. I wish to add a third; erring sons. Every son you father will land himself/ herself in trouble and you have to bring them out. Now, I know many leaders will tell you that they are too busy to bring restoration to sons that have fallen into trouble, and that the church board must deal with it. The truth is no one restores sons better than spiritual fathers. Jesus never passed Peter on to the board of Elders when he needed restoration. He restored Peter Himself in *John 21*. Why? Because restoration is such a personal an intimate thing that only the most trusted person in your life should be doing.

There are a few things a spiritual father does to ensure his sons become successful leaders.

"I pray for all my sons every day".
                                                    -Alfred Gerald Fabe

A spiritual father has an incredible advantage over fathers that do not know Christ. They have the privilege of accessing the greatest source of power and provision on behalf of their sons. We had the privilege of hosting Alfie and Lena Fabe in our house on a few occasions. Every morning he would repeat the same routine. He would get up early, brew the coffee, make sure that his wife had a cup of coffee in bed, and then he would pray. And as clockwork we would hear him mention the names of his spiritual sons before the Lord in prayer. The more sons he embraced, the longer his prayer time would be.

When we resided in Cape Town, I would speak to him nearly every day and every time I spoke to him, he would say, "I prayed for you this morning". Those words gave me tremendous courage to face the unknown vicissitudes of ministry with tenacity when things seemed to fall apart.

How do we pray for our sons? One of the great spiritual fathers in the New Testament was Paul and in every one of his letters we find him praying for the people he wrote to, bearing in mind that he also visited and ministered to them.

So here are some things you can pray over your spiritual sons and daughters based on the way Paul prayed for the churches in Asia minor.

- **Thanksgiving**. In nearly every one of his letters Paul gives thanks for the people he was writing to. What a privilege it was for Paul to be connected to each of those churches and also to each of those believers. Each believer represented a uniqueness that was valuable in building the kingdom, and Paul thanked God for them.

Colossians 1:3 *We always thank God, the Father of our Lord Jesus Christ, when we pray for you.*

- **Wisdom and Knowledge.** These are two important virtues that are so essential to living out the gospel. God gave Solomon a choice and he chose wisdom.
Colossians 1:9 *That's why we have not stopped praying for you. We have been praying for you since the day we heard about you. We keep asking God to fill you with the knowledge of what he wants. We pray he will give you the wisdom and understanding that the Spirit gives.*

- **Abundance of hope.** Our hope is in the Lord and it can be described as the confident affirmation that God will complete what he has commenced. It is not a wish. It is a steadfast assurance in our God who is Sovereign.
Romans 15:13 *May the God who gives hope fill you with great joy. May you have perfect peace as you trust in him. May the power of the Holy Spirit fill you with hope.*

- **Being filled with the Peace of God.** The enemy will throw many things at your sons and daughters to try to rob them of their peace. A lack of peace can so easily lead to a lack of hope and Paul knew that with the immense pressure the church was under in the Roman world, the only thing that would keep them sane under severe persecution was the peace of God.

2 Thessalonians 3:16 May the Lord who gives peace give you peace at all times and in every way. May the Lord be with all of you.

- **Strengthened with spiritual power.** The new church of the first century was characterised by the immense power that operated in every one of their lives. In **Acts 1:9** Jesus gave a promise that when the Holy Spirit is poured out upon God's people, they will be filled with divine power. That is the power they will need to carry out the commission of Jesus to the ends of the earth. *Ephesians 3:16 I pray that he will use his glorious riches to make you strong. May his Holy Spirit give you his power deep down inside you.*

- **To carry the presence of God.** There should be no greater joy for a father than the knowledge that his sons and daughters carry the presence of God wherever they go. I have made this part of the blessing that I impart on sons and daughters. I decree that wherever they find themselves they might know the presence of God active in their lives. The power of the Holy Spirit enables us to use our gifts so that salvations, signs, and wonders may result. The presence of God is the force that attracts people to Jesus even when we are not functioning. The more His presence is allowed to fill our lives the more like Him we become. We need both the power of the Holy Spirit and the abiding presence of God.
Ephesians 3:16 + 17a [16]that He would grant you,

According to the riches of His glory, to be strengthened with might through His Spirit in the inner man, ¹⁷that Christ may dwell in your hearts through faith.

- **To grow in the love of God.** Jesus gave a new commandment that sums up the law of Moses. That we love the Lord our God with all our heart, soul, and spirit and that we love our neighbours as ourselves.
  Philippians 1:9 And this I pray, that your love may abound still more and more in knowledge and all discernment,

- **To walk in righteousness and purity.** There has been much contention in the kingdom about righteousness. Some say it is a virtue we strive for every day. Others seem to contend that since we have already been made righteous through Christ, we don't need to strive for anything.
  Righteousness is something that every believer has to walk in. There is a distinction between us, and the world and it is called righteousness. Righteousness is the only thing that pleases God and not our gifts or our works. However, before righteousness can be walked out it must first and foremost be worked in.
  Righteousness must first abide in our hearts before it can be lived out in the streets.
  Philippians 1:9-11 ⁹And this I pray, that your love may abound still more and more in knowledge and all discernment, ¹⁰that you may approve the things that are excellent, that you may be sincere and without offense till the day of Christ, ¹¹being filled with the fruits of

righteousness which are by Jesus Christ, to the glory and praise of God.
2 Corinthians 13:7a *Now I pray to God that you do no evil.*

- **A heart of thanksgiving and praise.** The devil will readily give us reasons to be miserable and critical, but as Paul prayed for the believers in Asia minor, he constantly echoed the idea that all believers constantly be filled with praise and thanksgiving despite their circumstances.
  Ephesians 1:3 *Blessed be the God and Father of our Lord Jesus Christ, who has blessed us with every spiritual blessing in the heavenly places in Christ,*

"True fathers serve together with their sons".

-Alfred Gerald Fabe

This is one of those things Alfie firmly believed in. He loved serving with his sons. The trend is that sons watch their fathers but never get to serve alongside their fathers. There is no greater joy than getting your sons to accompany you on missions' trips. I have had the joy of taking some of my sons with me to numerous places both locally and internationally, and my greatest thrill was watching them function in their innocence and faith.

The New Testament contains tons of evidence of Paul and his sons travelling together for ministry.

In **Philippians 2:19-23** Paul tells the church that he plans to send Timothy to them and the only reason why he can do that is because Timothy has qualified himself by serving together with Paul. He served as a son with his father. There is nothing more precious in ministry than a son serving together with his father in the ministry.

As a second generation preacher I cut my teeth by serving together with my natural father. From as far back as I can remember, my parents were involved in ministry. They pioneered house church meetings all over Cape Town, and when I was able to play an instrument, I joined them and that became my weekly activity. From time to time, they would also spend a day preaching the gospel in rural communities and we saw hundreds of farm workers give their lives to Christ. That's indeed where I learnt to preach.

The reasons why serving with one's father is important is because:

- It is the safest environment for ministry. No father will allow any harm or embarrassment to come to his son.
- It is the best environment for learning. This is the way Jesus trained His disciples. They were on the road functioning with Him.
- It is the best way to ensure continuity in ministry. Fathers pass the baton of ministry to their sons, who in turn pass it to their sons. In this way, the ministry stays alive and more people hear the good news.

"The greatest accomplishment of a father lies not in what he attains, but in what he releases".

-Alfred Gerald Fabe

One of the serious questions that are normally asked about ministry, concerns the degree to which we measure the success of a tenure.

What are the marks of a ministry that has been successful?

- Does it have to do with the amount of people that follow the leader?
- Can it be determined by the number of people who are saved and baptised?
- What about the number of churches that are planted?
- Can it be based on the size of his intellectual property?
- Does a successful minister own a television network or a radio show or notable podcast?

We now know that it has nothing to do with the things he/she was able to amass or accomplish in their lifetime. So, how do we determine whether a ministry is being successful or not?

Business success is, for the most part, determined by influence, staff complement and profit margin. If that business is not influencing the market, growing their staff, nor seeing profit growth, then by business standards it is not successful.

Does the kingdom of God function that way? Certainly not, yet modern trends show that most churches consider numerically and financial growth to be the landmarks of their success. When you look at the New Testament you will find Jesus and the apostles demonstrating a new model that ensures growth and success.

Remember the early church that functioned after the day of Pentecost? Remember how the apostles wanted to keep the church in Jerusalem? That was contrary to what Jesus taught. He wanted the gospel to reach the ends of the earth, but with the church stuck in Jerusalem that objective would never have been reached. So, a great persecution took place that Eventually saw the church being scattered to Asia minor.

Something totally new starts happening in *Acts 13.*

There was in church in Antioch that was started as a result of the great persecution *Acts 11:19-25.*

The Jerusalem church heard about this and they sent Barnabas to Antioch. He was delighted by what he witnessed at Antioch. Lots of people were coming to faith in Christ. He decided to look for Paul, whom he found in Tarsus. He brought him back to Antioch and for a year they taught the church.

One day, at an appointed season in the life of that church, while they were fasting and worshipping, which seemed to be their custom, the Holy Spirit interrupted their meeting and instructed them to release Paul and Barnabas for the work of the ministry.

They fasted and prayed about that and, on a specific day, laid their hands on them and released them.

Here's the dichotomy. The Jerusalem church started as a direct result of the outpouring on the day of Pentecost. The church in Antioch started as a result of a scattering. The church in Jerusalem grew by leaps and bounds. In **Acts 4:4,** we are told that the church grew, and the number of men alone was 5000. The Greek word is *Andros* which means males. This does not include women and children. So, the number could easily have been 10000 people. That's a mega church according to today's standards.

The Church in Antioch was smaller, had no recognised apostolic leaders and yet became the prototype of a successful church. The leaders in Antioch understood that success was not measured by how many people they could retain, but by what they could release. No prize for guessing which was the most successful church in the end.

A good father ensures, that whatever he has raised up, gets released. His wealth is determined by what he releases.

This leads me to the next quote:

"Failure to father a successor is the cancellation of your own legacy".
-Alfred Gerald Fabe

Shannon Alder said: *"Carve your name on hearts not tombstones. A legacy is etched into the minds of others and the stories they share about you"*.

I have had the honour as a minister to conduct the dedication ceremony of many babies. In the latter years of my ministry, the dedication ceremony evolved into the pronunciation of the fathers blessing. As I held those babies in my arms to pronounce the blessing, the Lord would often ask me, do you know who this child truly is? I may have introduced them to the church by a specific first and last name, but the Lord knew their true identity.

When fathering sons, we often make the mistake of prematurely assuming their true identity and destiny. Consequently, we hold back on some and *over-impart* on others, yet as they step into their destinies the reverse effect happens. The ones we least expect often become the ones who make the greatest impact and vice versa. This should teach us never to hold back when fathering, regardless of our perceptions of a son.

Jesus spent three years imparting everything He had into twelve men and He didn't hold back. He was preparing them for the world in His absence. The most foolish thing any father can do is not prepare his son for the world of his adulthood. Also, he is guaranteeing an end to his legacy.

In Hebrew times, the day of a son's adoption was the day in which his father's legacy was inaugurated. From that moment on, everything a son learnt from his father, was going to be perpetuated, and if a father failed to dedicate his life to imparting those values to his son, then he was in reality cancelling his own legacy.

History is filled with the stories of great men and women who did much to affect society with their wisdom and contributions, yet they took those things to the grave with them, and never left their legacy in others.

"Name your successor".
-Alfred Gerald Fabe

A true spiritual father not only makes sure that his legacy lives on after him, but he also names the person who will succeed him in ministry. This is very important. The practise of naming a successor and mentoring that candidate for succession is not easily practised. Most denominations have different methods of appointing successors. The problem is that very often this appointment turns out to be counterproductive and the ministry suffers. That type of failure rarely happens when a minister names his successor, and now raises him/her up for succession. At an appropriate time (often determined after much prayer), the minister should make an announcement to his constituency of his intention to pass the ministry to a successor, whom he has mentored and now names. This succession or passing the baton should not take place when the minister dies.

I wish to suggest a simple formula for this process. In my teenage years at school, I participated in the inter-school athletic meetings. My personal favourites were short distance sprints and relay races. Our coaches knew how fast we could sprint and so they did not spend much time trying to make us run faster, rather they spent time helping us master the technical stuff like coming out of the starting blocks, staying in our lanes and the big headache of all, handing over the baton in relay races. We spent hours mastering the handing over technique. Most relay races are lost, not because the runners are slow, but because the hand over process is not good enough.

I wish to suggest a few things to leaders who want their sons to succeed them successfully. It is like passing the baton in a relay race.

- You have to be in the same lane. This may seem obvious, but I have seen teams lose a race because the officials placed team members in the wrong lanes. Fathers and sons need to be in the same lane. This means that their hearts have to be knitted together around a single vision. You cannot be running the same race in different lanes. During the mentoring process, the father makes sure that the son is not side-tracked by the methods and successes of other ministries. There has to be a single focus and the son must pursue that with everything he has.

- Before the baton is handed over the successive runner goes back a few steps so that he could gain speed and remain in his boundary when the hand-over takes place. They actually run together for a short stint at the same speed as the baton is passed from one runner to the next. No matter what the gifts or talents of the son are, he has to get to the place where he can reconcile with or accommodate the speed of the father.

When you read the story of Elijah and Elisha, you will notice that both of them performed the same miracle on the same day. In **2 Kings 2:8**, Elijah took his cloak, struck the water with it and the water parted. After he was taken up into heaven, his cloak fell on the ground and Elisha struck the water with the same cloak. The water parted the second time. Elisha was brought up to speed with his father and this was the evidence.

- After the handover, the first runner continues to run behind the second runner for short period egging him on. After a father has handed the baton over to his son, he doesn't abandon him, but stays with him for as long as it takes, until he is able to stand alone. He becomes his lifelong advisor.

There is an important detail I deliberately omitted. Who owns the baton?

A runner receives the baton and passes it to his teammate, but in reality, neither of them actually own the baton. No matter how big we grow the ministry, we are never the owners. Any ministry which has an earthly owner is not worthy of being passed on. This is the one thing the Lord has been dealing with me until now. He told me never to place the personal pronoun *"my"* before the word church or ministry. You may have started it and built it to have multiple campuses, but you don't own it. Jesus does.

Chapter six

Grab that towel.

Leadership is a topic that has been discussed more than any other issue today. It gets spoken about in the workplace, very often by disgruntled workers who feel like they've been unfairly treated by their superiors.

Political leaders constantly remain an object of debate, regardless of who they are. Church leaders are constantly under a magnifying glass. Leadership in any context will always be the focal point of much contention.

From the earliest days of the Bible, the enemy has been waging a war against leaders. As a result, millions of books have been written on the subject of leadership. Other works which focus on things like finance, sport, marriage, medicine, psychology, engineering etc will always have an underlying allusion to leadership. Fictional books will portray leaders as either being tyrants or heroes. No matter where one goes, leaders will always be required in every aspect of life and culture.

John Maxwell, the great leadership guru said, *"Everything rises or falls with leadership"*.

Good leadership therefore is paramount to every operation in life. Nothing will work without good leadership. Leadership played an integral role in the historical narrative found in the Bible. The Bible makes it clear that there were good leaders and bad ones.

The truth is that the world cannot continue to sustain itself without leaders. Someone needs to lead the charge in preparing the soil, planting the seeds, reaping the crop, and placing it on the market so that the people can thrive. The same can be said for every other thing under the sun. The animal kingdom submits to leaders like alpha males or alpha females, pack leaders and matriarchs. That is how they survive. When God formed the world, He had leaders in mind.

The problem with mankind is that we have corrupted the God idea and turned leaders into tyrants.

"The greatest act of leadership is fathering".
-Alfred Gerald Fabe

My spiritual father believed that leaders should function as fathers, because of its intimate nature and what it produces. I covered a lot of this topic in the previous chapter and the only thing I need to reiterate is the fact that leadership is most effective when done in a personal and intimate way.

It is a known fact that the maximum number of people a leader can impact in this way is twelve. Jesus demonstrated this in an impeccable way by sowing His whole life into twelve men, who in turn were to pour out their lives into others. While thousands followed Him and hailed Him as their leader, Jesus poured into twelve men like a father pours into his children.

The trap of the enemy is to make a leader go after big crowds so that he neglects the tremendous opportunity of pouring out his life effectively into the few.

Being a father to a generation will strip you of the pride and arrogance of the job title and coerce you towards a place of transparency, intimacy, and honesty. As a true father, the outward recognitions become unimportant as you literally lay down your life for your sons. I wish to iterate that not many leaders are prepared for this. So, the question arises, how does the Bible define leadership?

> *"Leadership is not about titles but about towels".*
>
> *-Alfred Gerald Fabe*

Leadership is a subject that is constantly under development. The world has seen different styles of leadership.
There are 8 popular styles of leadership being practised in society today.

- **Democratic leadership** - This style of leadership allows the leader to make decisions based only on the input of the members involved. It is extremely popular and commonly used in organisations where there is a board responsible for the running of the organisation.

- **Autocratic leadership** - This style of leadership is the direct opposite of democratic leadership. Here the leader makes decisions without the input of his team or board.

- **Laissez Faire** - This is a French term which literally means *"let them do it"*. There is a leader in charge, but he allows the people to make and implement all the decisions.

- **Strategic leadership** - This style of leadership gets the persons in charge to set the vision and even provide the resources, but then they allow the followers to own the implementation thereof. They are excellent strategists.

- **Transformational leadership** - Companies employ these types of leaders if they want to consistently implement change in order to precipitate growth. This leader constantly pushes his followers or employees outside of their comfort zones.

- **Transactional leadership** - This type of leadership style uses incentive programs to motivate followers. He may introduce a bonus whereby employees are remunerated if certain goals are attained. He forms a transaction with his followers / employees.

- **Coach style leadership** - This leader focusses on

finding the individual strengths or gifts of each member and then nurturing those attributes. Even though his objective is to see the company / organisation grow, he believes that when people grow and develop then the company will also.

- **Bureaucratic style leadership** - This type of leader tends to be democratic in style. He may listen to the input of the members. However, when that input transgresses the policy or past practises of his company then he will reject it.

These leadership styles are linked to a few things: our personality types, our training, our convictions, and the leadership style we submitted to.

There is another style of leadership which is closer to the Biblical example modelled by Jesus.

Servant leadership

In 1970 Robert K Greenleaf wrote a ground-breaking paper entitled *"The servant as leader"*, in which he contended for a style of leadership, which was influenced by his Judeo-Christian background. He was a retired A.T. & T executive, and his premise was that good leaders first needed to become good servants. Service needed to become the distinguishing factor of leadership, which in turn would create strong companies. He also felt that business leaders would find great joy in their lives if they raised the service aspect of their leadership and built more serving institutions.

What is unique about this style of leadership?

Well, to begin with, Jesus demonstrated this style of leadership in His ministry. The most notable example of this took place at the last supper in **John 13:1-17,** when Jesus took off His outer coat and wrapped a towel around His waist. After that, He poured water into a basin and began to wash the feet of His disciples.

I love the way Alfie Fabe said this: *"God Himself, the creator of the universe, took a bowl and some water and washed the feet of His disciples".*

Why was this practice important? He needed to meet a specific need that the disciples had.

Whenever guests were invited to a banquet they would generally travel on foot to the event. This meant walking on the same roads that were traversed by camels and donkeys. These roads were often strewn with dung, which inevitably became stuck to the sandals and feet of pedestrians. It was not uncommon that the living room would reek with the smell of camel's dung, and so as a sign of hospitality and a way to refresh each guest, the slave would be tasked with washing the dung off the feet of each guest. Now just reading this may cause you to gag, but that is what a slave had to endure every time his master had guests over for dinner.

What lesson was Jesus trying to convey? As a leader it is your responsibility to constantly serve your team. As you serve them, they become refreshed. When they join your team, their lives are often filled with spiritual and emotional 'camel's dung'.

Your interaction with them could either create more dung or wash it away.

The problem is that many leaders talk about serving their people, but their actions speak differently. They enjoy lording over people with a false sense of authority that comes with a warning not to *"touch the Lord's anointed"*.

Well, if Stephen was stoned, Paul was beheaded, John thrown in boiling oil, some of the believers thrown into an arena with lions, while other were covered with tar and set alight, what makes you and I so unique and untouchable?

Qualities of a servant leader.

Let's assume you are given the opportunity to attend a work-shop on leadership and your task is to identify the only servant leader in the group. What distinguishing qualities will you be looking for?

To begin with, Servant leaders are servants first. All you need to do is watch the demeanour of the crowd, and it will be easy to spot those whose sole objective is to serve. While others are discussing their accomplishments and the size of their group, the servant leader will be busy making sure the needs of the organisers and workers are met. They may even be packing chairs, carrying trays of food, and cleaning up afterwards.

Robert Greenleaf made this powerful statement in his famous essay.

"The servant-leader is servant first... It begins with the natural feeling that one wants to serve, to serve first. Then conscious choice brings one to aspire to lead. That person is sharply different from one who is a leader first, perhaps because of the need to assuage an unusual power drive or to acquire material possessions...The leader-first and the servant-first are two extreme types. Between them, there are shadings and blends that are part of the infinite variety of human nature.
The difference manifests itself in the care taken by the servant-first to make sure that other people's highest priority needs are being served. The best test, and difficult to administer, is: Do those served grow as persons? Do they, while being served, become healthier, wiser, freer, more autonomous, more likely themselves to become servants? And what is the effect on the least privileged in society? Will they benefit or at least not be further deprived? "

Let's discuss the criteria as well as some notable marks of servant leaders.

For anyone to function as a servant leader they will need to be:

- **Humble** - Servant leaders are not addicted to power, nor do they claim to have ultimate knowledge. In fact, they are willing to listen and learn from those they lead. They hold *1 Peter 5:6* in high regard. *Humble yourselves, therefore, under God's mighty hand, that He may lift you up in due time.*

- **Flexible -** Servant leaders are like putty in the hands of their masters. They learn to adapt to changing situations and have the temperament to deal with any curve ball thrown at them.

  When Paul wrote to the Philippian Christians, he was in prison in Rome. His entire Apostolic ministry was marked by changing circumstances. He had to adapt quickly to conditions that he did not plan for or foresee. So, in **Philippians 4:12-13** he said, *"[12]I know what it is to be in need, and I know what it is to have plenty. I have learned the secret of being content in any and every situation, whether well fed or hungry, whether living in plenty or in want. [13] I can do all this through Him who gives me strength."*

- **Virtuous -** Servant leaders are men and women with a high degree of moral rectitude. They intentionally hold themselves to a high degree of honesty and good character.

  Hebrews 13:18 *Pray for us. We are sure that we have a clear conscience and desire to live honourably in every way.*

- **Faithful stewards -** This is one characteristic that sets a servant leader apart from other leaders. While most leaders speak about managing time, money, resources and people, servant leaders use the word *'steward'* because they understand their total accountability to God who is the ultimate owner of all things. Everything they do is for the Glory of God and not their own. One of the great examples of faithful stewardship comes from the account of Joseph in Potiphar's house.

  Genesis 39:4-6 *[4]Joseph found favor in his eyes and*

became his attendant. Potiphar put him in charge of his household, and he entrusted to his care everything he owned. ⁵From the time he put him in charge of his household and of all that he owned; the Lord blessed the household of the Egyptian because of Joseph. The blessing of the Lord was on everything Potiphar had, both in the house and in the field. ⁶So Potiphar left everything he had in Joseph's care; with Joseph in charge, he did not concern himself with anything except the food he ate.

- **Compassionate** - Servant leaders see people the way Jesus sees them. One of the important lessons the disciples learnt from Jesus was to see people differently. While they saw people as being rebellious, Jesus saw them as sheep in need of a shepherd. A servant leader demonstrates empathy towards the people he serves.
1 Peter 3:8 Finally, all of you, be like-minded, be sympathetic, love one another, be compassionate and humble.

What are some distinguishing marks of a servant leader?

- Servant leaders understand that they function at the bidding of their master. They do not lead for self-gratification nor to seek special honour. They serve because they desire to bring pleasure to their master. Christian leaders must realise that they function only to bring glory to God.

John 7:18 *Whoever speaks on their own does so to gain personal glory, but he who seeks the glory of the one who sent him is a man of truth; there is nothing false about him.*

- Rather than seek their own promotion, servant leaders make the necessary sacrifices for the progress of others. The Christian world has seen too much of the reverse happen. In too many cases church leaders are the ones who become prosperous and gain positions of respect, while their people remain poor and dependant on their benevolence.

Philippians 1:25 *Convinced of this, I know that I will remain, and I will continue with all of you for your progress and joy in the faith,*

- Servant leaders willingly sacrifice their rights for the sake of the Gospel. Sometimes they give up their favourite hobby, sport or even meal for the sake of the Gospel. At least two of my colleagues made the decision to abstain from eating pork products for the sake of effectively witnessing to Muslims and Jews. What the other apostles called necessities, like having a believing wife, Paul was ready to sacrifice for the sake of the spread of the Gospel in Asia Minor.

1 Corinthians 9:5 *Don't we have the right to take a believing wife along with us, as do the other Apostles and the Lord's brothers and Cephas?*

- Servant leaders know when it's time for them to decrease. I am always amazed at the attitude of John the Baptist. Before Jesus started His ministry, John the

Baptist was the most notable Prophet in Israel. His message was the catalyst to the Gospel of the Kingdom, which came through Jesus. He had a growing ministry and many disciples. Everybody knew him. He was a man sent from God. He knew his message and his mission. Yet when Jesus appeared on the scene, instead of trying to make his voice louder, as many leaders do, he understood that it was now time for him to fade into the background.

John 3:30 *He must increase, but I must decrease.*

Leaders need to know when it's time to graciously bow out to a new era that God wants to institute.

The Pastor as Servant-Leader

One of the ways servant leadership should be clearly observed is in Pastoral care. The New Testament uses the Greek word *"poimen,"* which actually means shepherd, to describe a Pastor's role.

Throughout the Bible, we find shepherds looking after sheep. Moses was a shepherd, Joseph's brothers were shepherds, David was a shepherd when he was anointed to be king. Besides the fact that this was a common job in Israel, which the people understood very well, it becomes the only word used to describe a Pastor. The shepherd is a classic example of a servant-leader.

My eldest daughter Candice resides in Jaipur, India and she sent me this personal yet fascinating account of her interaction with a shepherd close to her home.

"There's a Shepherd that has approximately 100 sheep. He often leads his sheep to a grazing spot opposite my apartment. Now, one looks and sees that the sheep all obey the Shepherd. They know his voice. They follow after his voice and it doesn't matter what noise pollution is around, they only obey one voice. Now, this is a desert environment and grazing pastures are few and far between. This is also a bustling city with lots of traffic and chaos. He leads from the front and when he stops, they stop. But there are also times when he leads from the back. When he knows they are okay and safe, he depends on his sheep leaders to lead (he has a few) and he walks behind them among the weaker smaller sheep. This also happens when danger is lurking from the back. Now when he goes to a grazing area. He first scouts the area. He looks for snakes and other predators. He positions himself in the middle of the flock so that he can see in all directions, again he depends on the other sheep. The Shepherd is also always prepared.

On a few occasions an ewe in his flock would give birth while they were grazing. He was prepared. After she gave birth, he picked up the new-born and the mother who bled all over him and walked home. The interesting thing about the sheep is that they are not just mindless sheep following mindlessly after the Shepherd. The Shepherd has taught the sheep how to cross the road. Sometimes he is way ahead, and they are following, but they know where they are supposed to go, and they know to watch out for traffic. They don't become frazzled by the traffic.

I asked him one day why he doesn't wait for them to cross the busy main road. He said that when they were small, he used to stand with them at the crossing and wait but when they grew, they needed to learn to look after themselves. So, he would cross and wait on the other side and coach them over. Now he has stopped doing that also. They know how to cross. The lambs he ties to their mothers, so they are automatically taught.

I learned that day that leadership is all about being the servant, leading from the front and the back and all about getting dirty, but most of all, it's about empowerment. Many leaders want to be the sole leader. A true leader creates more leaders and Lightens his load."

The Bible describes Jesus as the Great Shepherd of the sheep. This is how Jesus used the metaphor of Shepherd to describe Himself.

John 10:11-18 *[11]I am the good Shepherd. The good Shepherd lays down his life for the sheep. [12]The hired hand is not the Shepherd and does not own the sheep. So, when he sees the wolf coming, he abandons the sheep and runs away. Then the wolf attacks the flock and scatters it. [13]The man runs away because he is a hired hand and cares nothing for the sheep. [14]I am the good Shepherd; I know my sheep and my sheep know me— [15]just as the Father knows me and I know the Father—and I lay down my life for the sheep. [16]I have other sheep that are not of this sheep pen. I must bring them also. They too will listen to my voice, and there shall be one flock and one Shepherd. [17]The reason my Father loves me is that I lay down my life—only to take it up again. [18]No one takes it from me, but I lay it down of my own accord. I have authority to lay it down and authority to take it up again. This command I received from my Father.*

Caring for the sheep was a shepherding duty that everyone understood fully. But Jesus didn't stop there. He mentioned a few other things that Shepherds do.

- He faces danger to protect his sheep. Wild animals and thieves roamed the countryside and sheep often fell prey to these.
- He knows each sheep. Sheep all look and sound the same. It is extremely difficult to tell sheep apart, yet the shepherd knows his sheep. He has identified each one and has interacted with each one enough to know what their specific needs are.
- His sheep know him. Because of his special individual care, the sheep form a bond with the Shepherd and can identify him in a group of people.
- The sheep also know his voice. This means that he has to continuously speak to the sheep. They may not fully understand his language, but they know what his voice sounds like and when they hear his voice they instinctively respond.
- The Shepherd has compassion for sheep that are not part of that pen yet. They may be sheep that have wandered away from their masters and are in danger in the wild countryside. He even rounds up those sheep and brings them into the safety of the pen, while comforting them with his voice. They too learn to know his voice.
- He sacrifices his life for the sheep. A Shepherd loves the sheep so much that he is ready to die fighting for the sheep.

That's how much Jesus loves and cares for His sheep, and when He ascended on high and released the gift of Shepherd upon the church, He was literally bestowing upon Pastors the grace to care for the sheep just like He did.

In **John 21,** we have the account of Jesus restoring Peter after he denied Him. After they enjoyed breakfast, Jesus asked him a tough question. Do you love me? Peter said: "yes, I love you". Notice what Jesus did. He did not do what couples normally do after asking their spouses this question. They usually use this question as a means to manipulate their spouse into buying something expensive or performing a huge task.

Jesus wasn't out to seek something personal from Peter as payment for denying Him. No, Jesus was only interested in what should be done for the sheep. He said to Peter, *"feed my sheep, care for my lambs"*.   In other words, if you honestly love me then be a servant leader to the church.

Chapter seven

The true nature of church leadership

The first part of my ministry was served in a denomination which did not fully subscribe to the gifts mentioned in **Ephesians 4:11**. *So Christ Himself gave the Apostles, the Prophets, the Evangelists, the Pastors, and teachers*

Many of our denominational leaders were dogmatic cessationists who did not believe that certain gifts of the spirit were for today. As a result, the only office they knew and ordained was that of a Pastor. All church leaders were called by that office regardless of their gift. The interesting thing is that there were leaders who could easily have been allowed to function exclusively in the other four gifts because they were exceptionally skilled in those areas, yet they were known by the title Pastor and expected to function as such. Our denomination sadly did not make room for the other gifts to function. The results were obvious. They produced a body of believers who were solid in scripture, but weak in their relationship to the Holy Spirit.

God wants every believer to have both.

But there was another weakness, I noticed with Pastors. We were not decisive enough to the point of leading our churches from the front. Pastors were governed by their congregation. We had vision yes, but by the time the vision had done the protocol rounds, it either become stale because of the time it took to be approved, or grossly weakened because of board amendments.

The truth is that people want to be led. Most people want to be led from the front and according to the scriptures that is how they should be led. So, in nearly every church there would be the constant battle over who the real leader was, and I have discovered that when a man/woman has been anointed by God with the gift of leadership, the quickest way to frustrate them is to restrict their leadership by suppressing their gifts. Leaders need to lead from the front.

Our Friday morning fraternity of ministers began to experience a corporate hunger for more of the power of God activated in our lives. Even though we knew what the missing ingredient was, we tried to arrive at that goal by means of our own doctrine, which we tried to tweak a bit. This debate and conversation went on for months and finally one of the senior men who had formally been a Pastor with a Pentecostal denomination suggested that we consult a senior leader in his former denomination. This wise man of God knew immediately what our problem was, and he wasted no time in telling us that we needed the baptism in the Holy Spirit. That day a group of Baptist ministers knelt on a carpet and we received the baptism in the Holy Spirit. That was a glorious day, for the power of the Holy Spirit started moving in my life in unprecedented ways. My preaching took on a new dimension. Signs and wonders started manifesting in our services. People were receiving miraculous healing and demons were being routed at the name of Jesus.

As the Holy Spirit began to empower the gifts of the spirit in my life, He also began to make me sensitive to other leadership offices that exist in the body of Christ.

Soon after I started my relationship with Alfie Fabe, I heard him make the following statement that revolutionised my life:

"Nowhere in the New Testament do you find the term pastor used as a descriptive word for a church leader".

-Alfred Gerald Fabe

Except for **Ephesians 4:11**, the word "pastor" is not found in the New Testament again even though the word shepherd is used a few times. The word is *"poimen"* in the Greek and it simply means *shepherd.* Now let's unpack that word in context. We know where that word comes from. Owning sheep in Israel was not an uncommon thing. Many people owned sheep. The Arabian Peninsula was not known for its fertile land. Most of it was classified as desert and so in most cases sheep did not graze at home. They were led to the hills around Jerusalem and often places far away. The sheep owners would employ shepherds who would take the sheep to the grazing places. Being a shepherd did not require excessive skill. They led the sheep to pasture and kept them safe and it was not uncommon for the youngest son in the house to be assigned that responsibility. He did not make his own decisions regarding the sheep, but was instructed by the sheep owner. That in a nutshell is what a Pastor does. He cares for the sheep.

He doesn't cast vision for the sheep, appoint other shepherds or decide where the sheep will graze. He simply follows instructions. So, how does the Pastor become the descriptive term for a role that far exceeds the capabilities of a shepherd?

It is obvious from this metaphor that Pastors should not be given responsibilities that exceed their shepherding roles. Of the five-fold ministry gifts listed in **Ephesians 4**, the office of Pastor seems to be the one that has the biggest dropout rate.

It is estimated that about 1500 Pastors leave the ministry each month for different reasons. 1 out of every 10 Pastors will actually retire while in ministry. The other 9 leave for various reasons. Could this dropout rate of Pastors be caused by the load of other 5 fold responsibilities that they were never meant to carry?

The case for Timothy

The church has for centuries used Timothy as the New Testament prototype of a Pastor. This may have come about since Paul calls him his son. So, because Paul wrote personal letters to Timothy and Titus (whom he also called his son), an assumption was drawn that these two men were Pastors. These letters are commonly known as the Pastoral Epistles, which they are not. So, because the letters were described in this way, they became the main resource used when training and instructing Pastors as church leaders.

So, was Timothy an Apostle?

We do know that Timothy was sent to lead the church at Ephesus, but does that mean he was a Pastor?   Let's look at some biblical evidence.
I Thessalonians 1:1 Paul, Silas, and Timothy, To the church of the Thessalonians in God the Father and the Lord Jesus Christ: Grace and peace to you.

In this verse Paul includes Timothy and Silas as the men from whom this letter comes to the church at Thessalonica. Then in *chapter 2:6* we find him saying this:

"We were not looking for praise from people, not from you or anyone else, even though as apostles of Christ we could have asserted our authority".

Who was he referring to?   Timothy and Titus mentioned in *chapter 1:1.*

This means that Paul recognised Timothy's apostleship. Besides Timothy being an Apostle, the Bible also uses the same Greek word, which describes an Apostle, to refer to the apostolic office of other characters in the New Testament.

- **Apollos** - 1 Corinthians 4:6-13
- **Epaphroditus** - Philippians 2:25
- **James** - Galatians 1:19
- **Barnabas** - Acts 14:14
- **Andronicus** - Romans 16:7
- **Junia** - Romans 16:7
- **Titus** - 2 Corinthians 8:23
- **Silas** - 1 Thessalonians 1:1; 2:26

So, if the word Pastor is not a descriptive word for a church leader then which word is?

The church is first and foremost apostolic.

For centuries, the church functioned under the wrong identity. The church for so long has been functioning pastorally and not in its true designation.
The church is supposed to be apostolic both in identity and function.

What is the difference?

Well, the word Apostle in the Greek language simply means *"sent one."*

The word "apostelos" is also a marine term denoting an admiral sent out with a mission. One of their tasks was to explore new territories for colonising.

In the first few centuries this is how the church functioned. Every member understood their Apostolic calling. They did not become stagnant but were on the move. They moved from place to place spreading the gospel.

The problem came when the church was redefined as being pastoral. When that happened, it lapsed into the idea that a Shepherd had been hired to look after them.

Notice the metaphor that is conveyed in the parable of the lost sheep in *Luke 15:4-7*. The Shepherd has 100 sheep and finds that one of them has gone missing. He leaves the 99 and goes after the missing one. When he finds the missing sheep, he throws a party and rejoices. That's what a pastoral church does. The Pastor leaves the people in the safety of the sanctuary and he himself goes in search of those who are lost.

In an apostolic church the people are trained and released to go in search of sheep, who do not belong to their pen. They bring them in and welcome them. Then the new ones are trained and released to do the same. This is apostolic ministry in action.

Having said that, it does not automatically mean that every member is an Apostle. There usually is one apostle whose assignment is to prepare the church for works of service, and as they all function together in obedience to the great commission, they become Apostolic in nature.

Notice something about Paul and Timothy's relationship.

In **2 Corinthians 1:1** we see this: *"Paul, an Apostle of Christ Jesus by the will of God, and Timothy our brother, to the church of God in Corinth, together with all his holy people throughout Achaia":*

Notice here how Timothy is first called our brother.

It is possible when **2 Corinthians** was written that Timothy was in training even though he was mentioned in the introduction. However, when we come to **1 Thessalonians 2:6** Timothy is now seen in a new light. Now, Paul recognises him an Apostle. What happened?

Timothy attached himself to Paul and as he did that, he himself grew into that Apostolic gifting.

So, how does a church become Apostolic?

Well, even before you make any transitional moves, the first thing is that you form a relationship with someone who functions as an Apostle. As you submit to their leadership an impartation will begin to take place and an Apostolic mantle will be released upon the church. People will soon realise that the old order of things is becoming obsolete and they themselves will insist on being transitioned.

I offer another verse to substantiate my point.

Mark 3:13-14 [13] *Jesus went up on a mountainside and called to Him those He wanted, and they came to Him.* [14]*He appointed twelve that they might be with Him and that He might send them out to preach.*

Jesus went to a solitary place for this part of His ministry. Luke's account says that He prayed all night, and in the morning, He called His disciples to Himself. Now, from these passages it is clear that the twelve were not the only disciples that Jesus called to Himself. There was a large group who were already following Jesus. So, He short-listed some of them and took them with Him to a mountain to pray. In the morning He called them to Himself and from that group He short-listed 12 men and designated them Apostles. So, Jesus sifted through the group twice until He found 12 and then He designated them Apostles.

This happened at the start of His ministry and not at the end. Usually, we would make that type of appointment at the end of a lengthy period of training and preparation, yet Jesus made the designation before any training happened. This is amazing, but there is a great truth to be learned here. God never calls those who first qualify for ministry. No, He qualifies those whom He has already called. He did not first watch the 12 to see if they met specific requirements. He called and designated them while they were still raw.

The exclusive purpose for the appointment lies in the rest of the sentence, *"that they may be with Him and that He might send them out"*.

Now the question is, when did these men start functioning in their full Apostolic capacity? From the day of Pentecost, after they were filled with the Holy Spirit. The fact that He designated them means that Apostolic authority was already bestowed upon them by virtue of their designation, but they only began to fully operate in that designation after He ascended.

The link between the designation and the operation was three and a half years of intimately walking with Jesus. An Apostolic calling does not take place after a man/woman has gone through Seminary and internship. No, it happens way before that. From the day you were born again you were designated for a specific task. The truth is that you probably didn't know it then, but as you walked with Jesus it became clear to you which direction He was leading you in, and your calling began to manifest itself and became apparent to you and everyone else.

Notice how His presence in their lives transformed them. A group of foul-mouthed fishermen started walking with Jesus and a band of powerful spirit-filled men of God emerged.

As we trace their ministry through the book of Acts, we are left with one conclusion.

"The dominant anointing in the book of Acts is the Apostolic".

-Alfred Gerald Fabe

I find it absolutely amazing how we can study the book of Acts, follow the Apostolic movements of the Apostles, teach the resulting precepts and principles, and then still decide that the church is Pastoral. How can that be, when the dominant anointing in the book of Acts is the Apostolic anointing?

Jesus did not designate 12 Pastors in **Mark 3:14**. If He

designated them Pastors then the church would never have left Jerusalem after the day of Pentecost, and quite possibly we may not yet have heard the Gospel. God's plan for the church was always that she be dynamic and not static. God is always on the move. Even though He never changes in nature and character, He never duplicates His methods. We always find God doing new and different things throughout the Bible. That is supposed to be the inherent nature of the church, yet we find ourselves following the same program year after year. No wonder we are experiencing the greatest departure by Pastors from ministry than has ever been recorded. May I offer my own reason? It is because we are trying to lead pastoral churches in an apostolic age.

"An apostle is a father".
-Alfred Gerald Fabe

I am well aware of the scripture in **Matthew 23:9** in which Jesus said: *"And do not call anyone on earth 'father', for you have one Father, and He is in heaven."*

Without going into a lengthy theological debate on the subject Jesus was not talking about the honouring of parents as the Bible instructs in various places. He was simply telling the crowds not to afford the same title, (Father) given to God when they pray, to men. When we pray to God as Father, we pray to the one who is our source of supply. Man, no matter how anointed, is not our source.

So, don't give man the same title that you give God.

Having cleared that up, there is a grace upon Apostles that allows them to function as surrogate fathers in the body of Christ. A surrogate father is a father who functions in the place of another father.

Apostles take up this fatherly role in the body of Christ. They rear the family of God on His behalf.

How do I know this?

Paul makes this statement in *1 Corinthians 4:14-15* "*I am writing this not to shame you but to warn you as my dear children. ¹⁵Even if you had ten thousand guardians in Christ, you do not have many fathers, for in Christ Jesus I became your father through the gospel*".

Notice how Paul says this: "*In Christ Jesus I became your father*".

He did not take ownership of those Christians. He did not boast that he gave birth to them.

He simply said that he became their father in Christ Jesus.

When we look at the fivefold ministry gifts in *Ephesians 4* then we immediately notice that all five of those gifts were contained in the life of Jesus. He embodied all those gifts. When He ascended into heaven, He released those gifts upon the church but unlike the gifts in *Romans 12,* which are received by the entire body, these gifts are only bestowed upon a few and no-one fully walks in all 5 of these gifts. We may have abilities in two or more gifts, but we really function in one of them.

So, just as the fivefold ministry are Christ centred gifts, in the same way fathering is Christ centred.

Jesus was our great Apostle and for three and a half years He fathered 12 men until they were able to function like Him and live out the legacy of fathering that He left them. Therefore, as an Apostle, Paul now approaches the church and tells them that they may have had many people who functioned as care-givers and nurturers (perhaps Pastors), but they did not have many fathers. He now became their father in Christ Jesus. Any minister who assumes to be a father outside of Jesus is a dangerous man. Do not follow him because he will control and manipulate you.

Notice, how Paul also calls Timothy his son at various places in the letters he wrote to him.

As a father an Apostle raises up sons and daughters so that they can eventually function in the same grace that was upon him. How does he do this? The way Jesus did.

He walks with them, imparts truth into their spirits, encourages and exhorts them, brings correction when there is error and discipline and restoration when there is erring. I have not found any institution that can restore a son as effectively as a father can.

A father loves a son differently than a mother. A mother's love will heal wounds, but a father's love will release destinies. For example, when a son errs, a mother will come and bind up his wounds, feed him and get him to rest. We all need that from time to time. A father, on the other hand, will restore the son, but will also correct his behaviour so that he never errs again.

Hebrews 12:7 *Endure hardship as discipline; God is treating you as His children. For what children are not disciplined by their father?*

Hebrews 12:11 *No discipline seems pleasant at the time, but painful. Later on, however, it produces a harvest of righteousness and peace for those who have been trained by it.*

A father also releases those he raises up. A father trains his sons to do everything he does, and when the time is right, he releases them to do that. I have already made mention of what happens at the age of adoption.

Fathers never keep their sons to themselves. Some sons will always abide with their fathers, but the rest will need to be released. This is how the kingdom is supposed to be extended.

The father was never meant to get on a private jet by himself and travel the world preaching the gospel with a staff of armour bearers and bodyguards. He was always meant to raise up sons alongside him as he preaches the gospel. This is indeed what Jesus did, and when it was time for Him to leave, He did so with full confidence that His sons would function just the way He taught them.

"True leadership is about continuity".
-Alfred Gerald Fabe

The only type of leadership, that ensures continuity until Jesus comes, is Apostolic leadership. A businessman can only ensure continuity as long as his company makes a profit. When the company collapses so will the leadership.

In the Kingdom on the other hand, Apostles will teach their sons how to function when they have resources and also when they have nothing. Apostolic leadership is not dependent upon finances. Even if the church building burns down, Apostolic ministry continues, because the scope of ministry supersedes local resources. Apostles are always global in their thinking. They think beyond the paradigm of the local church.

They are always thinking and praying about invading territories and going where no one has gone before. They enjoy blazing new trails and exploring new frontiers. That is why a true Apostle's ministry will never end. There will always be a son to pick up where he left off and to blaze new trails for new generations to follow.

Chapter eight

The kingdom and the marketplace

"Apostles don't talk about the church; they talk about the kingdom".
-Alfred Gerald Fabe

When Jesus, the great Apostle of our faith, walked this earth, His messages and teachings centred around one theme, the gospel of the Kingdom. The Kingdom of God was the focal point of everything that Jesus came to teach.

Matthew 4:23 *Jesus went throughout Galilee, teaching in their synagogues, proclaiming the good news of the kingdom, and healing every disease and sickness among the people.*

As much as Jesus is interested in blessing every local church, His primary focus is the extension of His Kingdom on earth.

The Kingdom of God is not a physical or geographic place but a domain. Simply stated, it is God's sovereign rule and reign in the hearts of men. When we acknowledge Jesus as Lord of our lives, by submitting ourselves to His sovereignty, we enter the Kingdom of God. That is why, when speaking to Nicodemus in *John 3:3,* Jesus made the new birth the only criterion for entering the Kingdom of Heaven.

As a matter of clarification, the New Testament uses both Kingdom of God and Kingdom of Heaven. Kingdom of Heaven is mainly used in Matthew's gospel because it was written for a Jewish audience. Kingdom of God appears in the other gospels. So, these terms are interchangeable.

When Jesus taught His disciples to pray, one of the first things He taught them to ask God for, was that His Kingdom come upon the earth. The New Testament also alludes to another kingdom, the kingdom of darkness. (*Colossians 1:13*)

Every person on the planet is part of one of these kingdoms. Either they are under the dominion of Satan or the rule and reign of God.

So, when Jesus preached about the Kingdom of God through parables, He was doing a few things:

- He was introducing another Kingdom to them by telling them how His Kingdom works.
- He was causing them to understand that they were not yet in His Kingdom.
- He was inviting them to be part of that Kingdom.

Can you imagine how this type of language was received by the political leaders of the day?

Herod ordered mass infanticide when Jesus was born because he felt threatened. He was afraid that if many Jews knew about this baby that was to be the king of the Jews, they might just start an insurrection and he may lose his political power.

Many Jews themselves misinterpreted His message, assuming that He was about to deliver them from the Romans. But that was not the mission of Jesus.

The Kingdom that He was establishing was a spiritual Kingdom and the spiritual legacy that He left His disciples was one that saw the expansion of that glorious kingdom.

This is the language of Apostles. Even though they may lead or be part of a local body of believers, their ultimate focus is not that group of people. Their passion is to see the Kingdom of God being established in the hearts and minds of men. That is why Apostles often focus on places where there has not been a strong Christian witness.

Dr. Rick Renner is a Bible teacher who lives in Russia with his family. He moved to Russia in 1992 when it was still called the Soviet Union. When he was first invited to Russia, he declined out of fear because he had heard about the persecution of Christians by the communist KGB. God began to speak to him and finally he agreed to go. His obedience caused him to develop a deep love and passion for that nation, which finally led him to relocate to Russia with his wife and three young children. Today he leads a thriving ministry there, and the Christians in the West call him the Apostle to Russia. He literally pioneered a ministry in a hostile country and introduced thousands to the Kingdom of God.

That is how Apostles think. They are not afraid of being uncomfortable and even being threatened. They enjoy living on the edge. They don't care where they sleep, what they eat or how dangerous it may become. Their passion is to see people being translated out of the Kingdom of darkness into the Kingdom of God, at any cost.

A preacher who travels in style with an entourage in attendance, lives in a five-star hotel, and raises an offering while never connecting with the local people is not functioning as an Apostle. That's just a celebrity preacher. True Apostles literally give themselves away. They often return from a mission with nothing but the testimony of new believers to show for their effort. That is how the Apostles of old lived.

1 Corinthians 11:22-28 [22]Are they Hebrews? So am I. Are they Israelites? So am I. Are they Abraham's descendants? So, am I. [23]Are they servants of Christ? (I am out of my mind to talk like this.) I am more. I have worked much harder, been in prison more frequently, been flogged more severely, and been exposed to death again and again. [24]Five times I received from the Jews the forty lashes minus one. [25]Three times I was beaten with rods, once I was pelted with stones, three times I was shipwrecked, I spent a night and a day in the open sea, [26]I have been constantly on the move. I have been in danger from rivers, in danger from bandits, in danger from my fellow Jews, in danger from Gentiles;

in danger in the city, in danger in the country, in danger at sea; and in danger from false believers. ²⁷I have laboured and toiled and have often gone without sleep; I have known hunger and thirst and have often gone without food; I have been cold and naked. ²⁸Besides everything else, I face daily the pressure of my concern for all the churches.

"The kingdom will be extended where the glory is manifested".

-Alfred Gerald Fabe

What sets us apart from all the religions and ideologies on the earth today? People can deny the existence of God, they can debunk our message as rubbish if they want to, they can discredit the idea of faith in God, but what they cannot do is deny what happens to them when the presence of God is manifested. All it takes for that to happen is a simple testimony.

One day Jesus sent out a group of people to some surrounding towns that He Himself was planning to visit. He warned them that the mission would be dangerous and that they would feel like lambs thrown among ravenous wolves. But He told them what to do.

Luke 10:8-9 *⁸Whatever city you enter, and they receive you, eat what is set before you; ⁹and heal those in it who are sick, and say to them, The Kingdom of God has come near to you.*

Now, Jesus had not yet died on the cross, and the outpouring of the Holy Spirit had not yet taken place, yet He was ready to have His kingdom manifest itself through the obedience of the disciples.

What made the difference?

The difference comes in the form of a promise that stands out in His strategy in verse 1. He was sending them out to towns that He Himself was going to visit. In a sense His intention was sending a signal out to demonic forces that He was heading that way. We all know what happened when Jesus entered the region of the Gadarenes. If that was possible then, imagine what is possible now, that the kingdom is alive and well inside us.

In the great commission (**Matthew 28**) Jesus updated that intention by telling His disciples that He would be with them all the time.

Matthew 28:19-20 *[19]Therefore go and make disciples of all nations, baptizing them in the name of the Father and of the Son and of the Holy Spirit, [20]and teaching them to obey everything I have commanded you. And surely, I am with you always, to the very end of the age.*

In **Luke 10** He followed them. We are not told how soon after. But, in **Matthew 28** He promised to accompany us. Can you imagine the power that we have inside us by virtue of that promise?

If the disciples saw miracles in **Luke 10**, imagine what God really wants to do when we step out in obedience to Him, and harness that divine indwelling presence every time we minister. It is the presence of the Lord that makes the difference and not our eloquence or giftedness.

When we speak of the Glory then we speak of the manifest presence of God. God desires that the manifest presence of Jesus be the only thing that saturates our very beings.

That is the singular thing that will confirm the authenticity of our message and make the opening petition in the Lord's prayer a glorious reality. Your Kingdom come; Your will be done on earth as it is in Heaven.

I believe that God so desires a duplication of Heaven's atmosphere to be earth's reality. Amid the current crisis and atmosphere of ungodliness that currently besieges the world, Heaven is waiting to invade earth though us.

Once we get to grips with this and allow the presence of God to truly manifest in us, then this next statement will become the new reality.

> *"Any gospel that does not work in the marketplace will not work".*
> *-Alfred Gerald Fabe*

For most Christians, the only place where the gospel is preached and taught is inside the walls of a sanctuary or a home. As we allow the manifest presence of God to become active inside us, the preaching of the Gospel will be moved to the marketplace. That is where the Gospel ought to be lived and taught.

Before I moved to Iceland, one of the greatest joys in my ministry was to join some of my friends at their workplace ministries. Below are two accounts of how this happened.

A deacon in our church worked at a postal depot where mail was sorted and prepared for delivery. One day he asked if we would come and pray in the building, because he was trusting God to start a lunchtime ministry there. He received the relevant permission and so we went. Because we only had access to the administration block, that's where we prayed. I remember walking down those corridors and asking God for a move of the Holy Spirit in that building. While the night shift staff worked, we declared the purposes of God over their lives. In the weeks that followed, he started sharing the Gospel with his co-workers and one by one they started to receive Christ as Lord and Saviour. Subsequently, he started a prayer group with those who were being saved, and consequently noticed the hunger in them to know the word of God. He then asked if I would come on a consistent basis and teach the Bible. So, I went, and I was amazed at how hungry these new believers were for the Word of God. While this was taking place, people were still receiving Christ almost on a daily basis, and the Bible Study group grew weekly. We had to move from one room to a bigger room all the time. Revival was beginning to flow in that workplace.

At a major clothing factory in Cape Town, a dear brother heard the Lord tell him to start a ministry among the workers. He stepped out in obedience and started lunch time meetings. I would often go and share the gospel there and oh what glory would be in that canteen. There were prayer groups active in the mornings before people stepped into the factory and by the time the lunch time meetings began the power of God was steadily moving. People were receiving Christ on a daily basis including Muslims and hardcore unbelievers. Now, at that time the South African government had entered into some trade deals with China that proved to be detrimental to the textile industry. Many stores selling only Chinese manufactured clothing were opening across the country. Because they were produced from cheap labour and sold inexpensively in South Africa, the textile industry started to experience a huge loss in demand. As the demand decreased many factories were forced to close. One day God gave this dear brother a prophetic word, so he went to the company CEO and boldly told him that because he agreed to have a Christian ministry in that factory, God would honour him, and he would not have to close his company like so many of his competitors were. God honoured His word and that company continued to generate a healthy profit.

Because of what the Lord was doing in that company he was now invited to start similar ministries at other companies. Soon we had the joy of commissioning him as a Pastor in the workplace. As those ministries were steadily growing, he eventually had to stop work so he could focus on the task of shepherding the 'workplace flock', keeping the fires of revival alive and pioneering new opportunities.

These stories prove that the Gospel works even more powerfully when taken outside of the sanctuary.

On the day of Pentecost, the disciples received power in the Upper room, but that power only became activated when they left the room and went to the marketplace. Perhaps every preacher of the gospel should test their message by taking it to the marketplace first before delivering it to the people on Sunday. If it works in the marketplace then it will certainly work in the church.

Darren Shearer from his book **"The Market place Christian"**, gives 7 reasons why the marketplace is a great place for Christians to be effective.

- **"Almost all non-Christians are in the marketplace".** Think about that. It is a known fact that Church attendance is dropping fast. People are leaving churches for various reasons, yet that same people are waking up each morning and going to work. Should we not be reaching people where they are?

- **"Almost all Christians are in the market".** The Pastor and paid members of staff may be the only people who don't experience the marketplace on a daily basis. The rest do.

- **"Discipleship can actually happen in the marketplace".** The Christians in the marketplace can actually disciple the unbelievers where they are. True discipleship is not taught in a classroom but demonstrated first before Christlikeness is influenced.

- **"The marketplace is a more authentic showroom of Christianity".** This is where unbelievers get to see if the Gospel truly works or not.

- **"The marketplace forces the church to use all of its capabilities".** Only a few people can exercise their gifts in the sanctuary at any time and the rest are spectators. In the marketplace however, the only spectators should be the unbelievers. The marketplace gives every believer the opportunity to be effectively used by God.

- **"Denominational divisions are less destructive in the marketplace".** The marketplace seems to be the place where all Christians become united around a common cause. It is there that all our theological differences become irrelevant.

- **"Everything gets funded from the marketplace".** The strength of the marketplace determines the strength of a nation's economy and if business leaders are reached with the Gospel, they will begin to make righteous decisions concerning the channelling of their money.

So, what happens when the marketplace is reached?

> *"When you take the marketplace, you take the city".*
>
> *-Alfred Gerald Fabe*

God is a God of the city. Throughout the Bible we see the unfolding of God's plan for reaching entire cities. He loves cities and invites us to be part of His plan to reach cities.

It is naive to talk about taking the city for Christ while ignoring the marketplace. The city will never be reached purely by having meetings in a sanctuary. Every vision to reach a city must include the marketplace. So, if the marketplace is key to reaching the city, then should marketplace ministry not become the main thing we do?

Ed Silvoso made a statement which revolutionised my thinking. *"When you Pastor a church, you Pastor a city".* Somehow Pastors were led to believe that the group of people who met in a sanctuary were their sole constituency. This could not be further from the truth. God has never designed a local church to be the ultimate vision for ministry. The fruits of any ministry must be seen in the marketplace.

The Kingdom of God cannot be confined to communities of believers in a city that meet on a Sunday morning. It has to reach the marketplace. The marketplace is crucial in the spread of the Kingdom, as an entire generation of irreligious people need to experience the reality of what the Lord taught us to pray: *For yours is the Kingdom, the Power, and the Glory, forever and ever. Amen.*

Chapter nine

2020 and beyond

The prophet Isaiah was used by God to speak to Israel. He told them that God was going to judge their unfaithfulness, after they had suffered punishment for their sin, He would restore them. He and other prophets carried a huge responsibility upon their shoulders because of the message they bore and their ability to hear God's voice.

I have often wondered what the defining moment of their calling was.

For Ezekiel it happened when he stood among his exiled people, along the banks of the Kebar river and received visions from God. The children of Israel were in captivity in Babylon, and they would often retreat to the riverbanks in Babylon to lament and cry out to God. It was on one or more of those occasions that he received these visions which led to the messages in the book named after him.

For Jeremiah it happened in chapter one, when God told him that He called him, even before he was born, to be a prophet to the nations. God tested his prophetic calling by asking him what he saw, and when he described in accurate detail the picture God was showing him, the call of God was established.

For Isaiah it was different. The defining moment happened in chapter six and was marked by the death of King Uzziah. It was in that same year, when the nation was dealing with his death and transitioning to the reign of Pekah, that Isaiah had a vision of the Lord in the temple. It was in that vision that he heard the Lord calling him to go and prophecy to the nation.

The church likewise has had many defining moments.

The great persecution of the church in **Acts 7**, after the stoning of Stephen, was a defining moment.

The day Martin Luther nailed his theses on the door of the Wittenberg Castle was a defining moment which triggered the great reformation.

Every major movement in Christendom had a defining moment or season.

In fact, when the New Testament talks about seasons the only word it uses in this context is the Greek word *"kairos",* which speaks about a defining season, an opportune time, a time designed by God.

The year 2020 has been that defining season for the church. While many expressed their disapproval at the way their visions were side-tracked by a pandemic, most will openly admit that this year has been defining in many ways.

- It caused many Christians to revisit their walk with God and make critical adjustments to their personal devotional lives. With so much time on their hands, they have been led to spend more time studying the scriptures and speaking to God.

- It brought the church back to the drawing board. Suddenly church leaders began to realise, that if they were to keep their people edified, their methods needed to change. As a result, many used social media as the platform from which to preach the gospel. It seemed impersonal at the time, but people got used to it.

- It caused people to define what was important. Suddenly around the world things were exposed which were previously hidden. The plight of the hungry and homeless was highlighted again. Domestic abuse multiplied as people were confined to their homes. Leaders around the world were forced to take a holistic look at these things and start addressing them.

- Christian leaders are realising that ministry will need a totally different approach, post COVID 19. Because things are changing so fast both domestically and politically, the way we did church in the past will become redundant.

A few years ago, we started sensing an urgency in Alfie Fabe's message to ministers. He looked at the deteriorating atmosphere over nations and made this statement:

"We have to get the job done".

-Alfred Gerald Fabe

We sensed the urgency in his voice and often he would break down and weep because of the state of the nations without Christ. This was one of the last things he said to me. *"Ron, we have to get the job done".*

I believe there is a divine mandate upon this generation to do just that. Over the past 50 years or so, God has provided just about every tool we need to get the job done. As He restored relevant gifts back to their rightful order, He also provided technological advances plus a wide range of platforms that will allow even the most incapacitated Christian to share the gospel.

The truth is that one does not need to be trained or ordained. Posting a scripture verse to a friend is as powerful as preaching a sermon. The only criteria are obedience. If you can type on your phone, then you can be used by God. It has become that simple.

Jesus made a simple yet profound statement in **Acts 1:9** *"But you will receive power when the Holy Spirit comes on you; and you will be my witnesses in Jerusalem, and in all Judea and Samaria, and to the ends of the earth".*

More sermons on missions and evangelism are preached from this verse than from most similar statements in the Bible, yet in most cases those who preach this are guilty of holding back those who wish to experience its fulfilment.

There are absolutely no criteria in scripture, other than being unsaved, that should prevent a believer from fulfilling this statement in its entirety. The only thing stopping people from fulfilling the great commission is the church.

I believe from the moment a person comes to Christ they should be introduced to the great commission. When a person gets radically born again, the Holy Spirit comes and lives within them. I use the word 'radical' because not everyone who prays the sinner's prayer is truly born again. That genuine New Birth experience is so radical that they begin to see the world with new eyes. Suddenly, they want to tell their friends and evangelize the world, and the church has gone to great lengths to stifle that.

We first introduce them to a 10 week new converts program, followed by a 15 week discipleship program, and then a compulsory evangelism and church planting program lasting 12 months. By the time we are done pumping knowledge into them we have also been successful in deprogramming them. Whatever the Holy Spirit placed inside them at conversion is now programmed out of them. Their passion dissipates, their desire disappears, and they become educated socialites.

God did not place that zeal inside them for nothing. It is there because it is supposed to be harnessed and utilized.

Take them on evangelism trips. Get them to share their testimony. Teach them how to preach while on the mission field. We were not supposed to clean them up before sending them. This is all part of the same process. Jesus did not say, the truly disciplined will receive power when the Holy Spirit comes upon them, and after they have graduated, they will be my witnesses, first in Jerusalem, for 5 years at least, and after they have knocked on every door, they shall try Samaria and then Judea, and just before they die, they will go to the ends of the earth.

This may sound funny, but it is exactly what we have done with new converts.

Papa Fabe had one rule, which I took too long to grasp. If a believer has a passion for a particular city or nation, then he / she needs to be released to go. Now, obviously nobody was released to go alone. People always travelled in ministry teams, which still is the safest and most powerful experience for a new believer.

For centuries, the universal idea of going to the nations involved a single man / woman travelling to a foreign nation on their own to live there permanently. In the last 30 years that picture has changed.

I remember attending a couple of missions conferences in South African in 1995 and 1996. The highlight on both occasions was the commissioning service at the end, where hundreds of young people, many of them teenagers, were set apart for short term trips around South Africa and to the neighbouring states. There was a tangible and dynamic energy that characterised those events as those young people, many of them new converts, with no sense of "Christian dress code", rejoiced and wept at the prospect that our Great God would esteem them so high to be used in all their simplicity.

Jesus desires that the Gospel of the Kingdom reaches the entire world, and He is ready to use *whosoever* avails themselves.

We have to get the job done.

The year 2020 is known for many things. It's been a year of decision making, transitioning, evaluating, and putting lives and homes in order.

As COVID 19 restrictions caused the churches to postpone their meetings indefinitely, some saw this as the greatest disruption of the ministry, while others decided to listen to the Lord and try to understand what He was saying.

At the same time Alfie Fabe decided to start preaching on Social media, which he did for many weeks until he was called home. This next statement will describe how he saw the situation.

"The devil mocked God and said: "see I have closed the churches, God told the devil, you may have closed church buildings, but I opened up churches in every home".
-Alfred Gerald Fabe

Many of our colleagues became irritated at the prospect of postponing their services and not being able to receive tithes and offerings, but Alfie looked at the opportunity that the church was being presented with. Too many times we expend all our energy focussing on closed doors when, if we would just reposition ourselves, we may actually see new doors opening somewhere else.

It is quite interesting that the very chair he sat in when he made that statement, was the same chair he sat in when he waited on God in prayer every morning for that new open door. What an example of repositioning.

So many of us think that we have to leave home and go to the mountains to hear God speak. If that works for you, wonderful. Please don't stop. However, for the rest of us the great repositioning happens between our ears. Our mindset becomes the greatest hindrance to discovering an open door. So, the greatest repositioning we need to make is the repositioning of our hearts.

When the Israelites were going through a season of repentance in the book of Joel, they were doing what people traditionally did when they were mourning and repenting. They tore their clothes. This was an outward sign of what was happening inside. But just like so many of us today who prefer rituals over reality, they replaced true repentance with an outward ritual and expected that to appease God. Truth be told, they had not changed one bit. This is when Joel realised the emptiness in the ritual and said in ***Joel 2:13*** *"Rend your heart and not your* *garments. Return to the LORD your God, for He is gracious and compassionate, slow to anger and abounding in love, and He relents from sending calamity."*

God delights in changed hearts not torn garments. Unless we are ready to have our hearts renewed, we will never see things through the eyes of Jesus and be open to a new strategy in a new season.

A renewed heart is the first step to repositioning ourselves, and the defining moments are seldom pleasant. They are usually accompanied by crisis of faith moments, that cause us to slow down or even come to a grinding halt, so that we have the time to deal with things that take us out of position.

What is your heart telling you in this season?

One of the things I believe God is saying comes from this next quote:

> *"God called you to build an army not an audience".*
>
> *-Alfred Gerald Fabe*

We are living in a war zone. Many contend that we are about to fight the final battle before Jesus comes back. How much longer before that happens, we do not know. What is important is that we get involved in the fight that is set before us.

There is a warrior spirit that God wants to develop in every believer who waits for His appearing. Wars are for warriors not wimps and God has called us to be soldiers not spectators. We have to get into the fight.

The only problem is the fact that soldiers are developed not born. It takes great skill to be a warrior and that skill is developed over a lengthy period of time.

Leaders have been commissioned by God to build an army of men and women, who will stand and face the enemy, toe to toe, like two boxers in a ring.

I love this passage in *1 Samuel 22:1-5* *[1]David therefore departed from there and escaped to the cave of Adullam. So, when his brothers and all his father's house heard it, they went down there to him. [2]And everyone who was in distress, everyone who was in debt, and everyone who was discontented gathered to him. So, he became captain over them. And there were about four hundred men with him. [3]Then David went from there to Mizpah of Moab; and he said to the king of Moab, "Please let my father and mother come here with you, till I know what God will do for me". [4]So he brought them before the king of Moab, and they dwelt with him all the time that David was in the stronghold. [5]Now the prophet Gad said to David, "Do not stay in the stronghold; depart, and go to the land of Judah". So, David departed and went into the forest of Hereth.*

David had just killed Goliath and as a result had been hailed louder than Saul. Since David was just a shepherd and Saul the king of Israel, jealousy overtook him, and he tried to end David's life. David then escaped the palace and was on the run for a while before landing in a cave called Adullam.

Soon afterwards his family got wind of this and they followed David to the cave, as well as men of Israel that were in some or other position of disenfranchisement. Among them were those who were in distress, those in debt and those who had become discontent. One can only imagine what the cave sounded like when this group of dysfunctional people entered. Some were complaining, others muttering, some may have been verbally venting their anger and the rest just gossiping.

That's usually what a mighty army looks like on admission day.

In fact, the very people who disqualified David, his family, led the group. What a mess.

Well, David had two options. He could join these people in the great pity party, or he could take what landed in the cave and transform it into something useful.

Thank God he chose the latter. These men stayed with David and he developed them into a group of highly skilled fighters.

Have you noticed that God never chooses the wise, highly skilled, educated and mentally healthy to be His first choice. He seems to deliberately go for those who are the most unlikely. Those whom society disqualifies and abandons. God finds them and raises them up to be His warriors.

We are not sure how long they were in the Cave, but according to verse 2 they were there long enough for David to become their captain. He took a bunch of losers and developed an army.

The people that God places alongside you, whether they are children, teenagers, or adults, educated or unlearned, strong, or weak, qualified, or not, are your army and not your audience.

You have lots of things to say to them and they will be listening attentively to every word, but you also have the divine assignment to get them mentally fit, spiritually sensitive, and skilled in the use of spiritual weapons because the time for war is upon us.

Chapter ten

"Ya'll come back now".
                                        -Alfred Gerald Fabe

Should missions be long term or short term? This question solicited lots of debates throughout the centuries. Some Missiologists contend that world mission cannot be short term because of the time it takes to learn a language, engage a culture, and earn the trust of the people. However, there seems to be a shift taking place in world missions. Over the last 30 years the world of missions and evangelism has undergone lots of changes. People have access to all kinds of information and the English language has become the most common language spoken all over the world. In fact, one hardly finds a country where English is not spoken at least as a second or third language. It seems that the emphasis has shifted from long term missions to short term stints. This does not mean that long term missions have ended or become obsolete. There still is a place for people who feel the call of God to leave the place of their birth and go to a land the Lord directs them to, for the purpose of making a long term investment of their lives, which usually has no end date attached to it. Many people groups could only have been reached that way.

However, this traditional way of doing missions has not seen more of the Ekklesia being released for foreign ministry.

Today we talk about short term trips in which groups of people are taken into regions for anything from a day to a few weeks. In those few weeks they are intensely involved in ministry which usually happens all day every day. They would have meetings in the mornings and evening with outreaches during the afternoon.

I remember taking some of our church folk on such a trip to Mozambique in 1996. The country had been war ravaged and the infrastructure was still in a state of disrepair. Bullet holes in building walls were visible and the roads still had huge potholes made by explosive devices and combat vehicles. The war was over, but there was still a state of hopelessness that existed in the hearts of the people.

We arrived at our host church while the morning service was still in progress. It was a rainy day, and the congregation was huddled together in a few corners of the sanctuary. We immediately noticed why. The roof had huge holes in it and rain was pouring into the building just as profusely as it was outside. It was in really bad shape.

We collected all the extra cash we could from the group, bought materials, and one of our team members worked tirelessly to fix the holes in the roof. By the end of that week that roof was repaired, and the church could comfortably meet in that building again.

There were a few young people on that trip who were skilled in performing arts and during our morning outreaches they would stop on random street corners and perform short skits to draw a crowd, after which there would be a short gospel message, followed by an invitation to receive Christ. People eagerly responded to the gospel message and we led hundreds to faith in Christ.

One of the highlights of the trip came while the team was sharing the gospel in a village. As they walked, two by two, from house to house, they noticed a woman watching them intensely. They would enter a house and then leave after fifteen or twenty minutes. When they left the hosts would come out to bid them goodbye with a joy on their faces that she had not seen before. There was laughter and hugs, which was new to her. She had not seen them this happy. The truth is they were all receiving Christ as Saviour. She realised that they had something that she desperately needed, so she ran down the road to two team members and stopped them before they could enter another house. She fell on her knees before them and asked them to please give to her what they gave to her neighbours. They immediately shared the gospel with her and led her to faith in Christ. Obviously, these young people were in tears and humbled by this experience and the rejoicing in the team was great. Can you imagine how the angels felt?

We saw signs, wonders and miracles being performed by the Lord and He was using these young people in amazing ways. To many of them this was their very first outreach.

Short term mission teams are a great way to get people from the pew to the field, and in the years I served the churches of Kingdom Ministries International, we had the joy of commissioning short term mission teams multiple times a month.

We have to move the people from the pew. The pew may be the place of their greatest learning, but it can also become the place of their greatest stifling.

"Most churches are after seating capacity and not sending capacity "

-Alfred Gerald Fabe

In the previous chapter I discussed the idea of building an army not an audience. Ever since the institutionalism of the church, in the fourth century under Constantine, the desire for invading territories with the gospel of Jesus seemed to wane, until the church finally went to sleep and entered the dark ages.

One of our seminary lecturers once said that when a church does not involve itself with the great commission then it will be embattled in all kinds of internal and external conflict. The truth is that the Great Commission is a battle.

Paul said in **Ephesians 6:12** *"For our struggle is not against flesh and blood, but against the rulers, against the authorities, against the powers of this world's darkness, and against the spiritual forces of evil in the heavenly realms"*.

This was part of the closing chapter of Paul's letter to the church at Ephesus. One gets the sense that he is remembering some of the things that they have been struggling with as a church and he quickly addresses things like, the roles of marriage partners and the way slaves and their masters should interact, before proceeding to another important matter. He tells the church to be strong in the Lord and to make sure that they put on the armour of God. Now, he is not saying that some of them will be facing battles, instead he confirms what they all have been experiencing.

Ever since the day of Pentecost there has been a battle waged between the Kingdom of God and the kingdom of darkness and that battle involves every Christian. The kingdom of darkness seeks to destroy the Kingdom of God and vice versa. Every Christian born into the Kingdom of God inherits that warrior DNA and as long as we are involved in spreading the Gospel, the battle will always be waged on those fronts.

The interesting thing is that after the church was institutionalised the Christians got involved in other battles.

Here are some theological heresies that arose during that time.

- **Arianism (AD 318-451)** This was a denial of the divinity of Christ.
- **Nestorianism (AD 428)** This was the belief that Jesus was the adopted son of God and not the begotten Son of God.
- **Pelagianism (AD 400)** It was a doctrine of works and a rejection of the Grace of God for salvation.
- **Macedonianism (AD 362)** This was a denial of the divinity of the Holy Spirit.

Notice how these heresies twisted the message of the Gospel.

By the turn of the first Millennium the church got involved in another battle. The age of the crusades had arrived, and the battle now became physical. Islam had fast expanded as a religion and had conquered much of the middle east. The purpose of the crusades was to keep Islam at bay, to conquer paganism and retake control of the Holy Land. This was a dark time for the church.

The main problem was that church leaders were now enamoured with getting people into a single building for worship, during which time heresies and all kinds of other conflicts arose.

God was never interested in how many people we can squeeze into a building or how many campuses our church has. If our chief mission is to constantly extend our buildings or look for bigger ones to accommodate the crowds then we are not necessarily fulfilling the great commission.

What we do with those people after they join our church is what God is interested in.

My contention is that the true size of any church is not determined by its seating capacity but by its sending capacity. God's commission to the church was never to stay in one place. There is a reason why Jesus said "go".

We have to develop not only a sending paradigm, but we also have to adopt a sending strategy.

An Apostolic church is a sending church.

The next section serves as a caution to us as we go.

"Don't go where you are tolerated, go where you are celebrated".
-Alfred Gerald Fabe

Here is an important key to ministry. Sometimes we toil and toil for years in an area without any results. Now, I do believe that every seed we sow will bear fruit eventually, but sometimes it takes many years before any fruit is shown. I have heard many stories of people going into areas where they were not welcomed. They preached there anyway, and the results were negative. The truth is they may not have been obedient to the voice of God but decided to go anyway. Some of them left in personal disgrace and others left a trail of destruction behind them.

Sometimes churches will tolerate preachers but will not want them back again, and most times it has nothing to do with their message but with their behaviour.

One of the reasons I live in Iceland today is because of the way we were received when we first came here. We were well received by both the leaders and the people and over the years, God honoured us by opening doors that should have been closed to us. Sometimes we still marvel at the favour we received when coming to live here.

I have been in countries where other leaders have visited prior to me, and the general consensus of the people was that we should not allow that leader to go back to them. That was embarrassing.

The word 'celebrate' in the opening statement is simply used for the sake of rhyme. I prefer to use the word "honour".

The point is that honouring in a foreign nation should never be seen as a personal accomplishment.

Do not boast when people celebrate you. This is simply the open door that you have been praying for. The truth is that the world does not know how to celebrate Christ. Their eyes are blind, and their minds darkened, but they have met you and unbeknown to them, they are attracted to the Jesus in you. Jesus is always attractive in His nature. So, when you see people celebrate you then it simply means that God has opened a door.

The onus now is upon you to walk through that door with love, humility and the fruit of the spirit, and the way you conduct yourself will determine whether that door remains opened or closed.

In *1 Corinthians 19:7-9* Paul is speaking to the church and relating some future plans including his desire to visit them again. *⁷For I do not wish to see you now just in passing; for I hope to remain with you for some time if the Lord permits. ⁸But I will remain in Ephesus until Pentecost; ⁹for a wide door for effective service has opened to me, and there are many adversaries".*

It was obvious that he had great favour in Corinth. The people loved him, and he loved them, and he really wanted to spend some good quality time with them, but the Lord opened a door in Ephesus, even though there were many adversaries.

When we speak about being celebrated in a region, we are not discounting the possibility of opposition. There will always be opposition. We experienced great opposition in Iceland amid the favour that we walked in.

The enemy hates you and desires to see you fail. Opposition, however, should never deter anybody from persevering in a region. Jesus was often opposed where He went. There were times people wanted to kill Him. In the region of the Gadarenes, He was asked to leave. In Jerusalem He was lauded and then condemned just a few days later.

It is obvious that there was some kind of honour that Paul received in Ephesus. Perhaps it came from the Christians of the diaspora. However, he saw this open door and decided to walk through it and the rest is history. Even though Paul ended up in prison in Ephesus, a great church was established there.

Just like the sons of Issachar, Alfie Fabe understood these times and knew that God was preparing the nations for a global harvest of souls, and that it why he made this next statement.

"Apostles need to release Evangelists to the nations so they could reap the end time harvest with signs and wonders following".
                                        -Alfred Gerald Fabe

God is in the business of using the most unlikely people for His glory and after three decades of ministry I am convinced about one thing. The only criterion for being mightily used by God is obedience.

Very often we look at the lives and ministries of popular Evangelists and we assume that they have acquired something beyond their calling which is the catalyst to the harvest they reap. Now I know many of them would like you to believe that, but if they are brutally honest then they will tell you that the main ingredient was their obedience. I believe God always rewards obedience.

Think about some of those characters in the Bible who were no one's first choice for greatness, yet God took their obedience as raw material and created mighty warriors.

Gideon would not have been anyone's first choice. He was timid, fearful and when the angel found him, he was threshing wheat in wine press, where no one could see him. Yet God saw him and chose him.

Jonah was sent to evangelize an evil city and he did what most Christians probably would do. He tried to escape. God pursued him and after negotiating a fierce storm, being thrown overboard, landing up in the belly of a fish and then being spewed out along with the stomach contents of that fish, he finally made it to the city he was sent to, and the rest is history. The entire city was revived.

I marvel at the grace of God upon his life. God could have destroyed him because of disobedience but His grace showed him what happens when ordinary people obey. God used him just as powerfully as He had planned in the first place.

There is nothing that replaces obedience.

Alfie Fabe has a natural son that has also stepped into ministry. In 2004 before he made that decision, he accompanied his dad, Alfie, on a mission's trip to Rwanda. His role was just to be with his dad and learn. However, on the second day he noticed a meeting in a building close to the host church and there were about 200 ladies in attendance. They were being addressed by two men. Upon a closer look he noticed how unruly some of them were and he asked the interpreter why they were displaying this kind of behaviour in church. To his surprise he was told that this was not a church meeting, but that these were prostitutes being addressed by two government officials. Apparently, the government was busy with a reform program and wanted to get these ladies involved in alternate projects. Without thinking he asked the interpreter if he could speak to these ladies. The interpreter went to ask the coordinators and because he was a foreigner, he was given a few moments to speak. He had never preached before but with lots of trembling he shared the love of Jesus with that group and invited them to receive Christ. Before he knew it, half the crowd was kneeling at the stage and in tears gave their lives to Christ. This was a miracle which astounded the ministry team as well as the organisers of this meeting. The next year, two of those ladies launched a ministry to prostitutes.

Because Apostles are people with a mission, to see the gospel reach the ends of the earth, they are skilled in finding people who share that passion, so that they can raise them up and release them.

Alfie Fabe's desire was to see hundreds of Evangelists go from Cape Town to Cairo and then to the rest of the world. He spent his last days urging Apostles to ensure that Evangelists get released for that end time mission.

There is no greater thrill than to be on assignment for God and there has never been a more suitable time than now. The nations of the world have been pillaged by pestilences, wars, corruption, and unspeakable suffering. Slavery has taken on a new image involving women and children. The blood of the martyrs still lies fresh on the ground. Poverty and hunger have escalated to new heights.

Governments are fast losing hope of salvaging the peace and prosperity their nations once knew. The only thing that will bring hope to nations is the message of the Gospel and God has decided to use the most unlikely people for this assignment. I call them His secret weapon.